C000156228

A Gift for the Queen

(*Toḥfa-e-Qaiṣariyyah*)

By

Ḥaḍrat Mirza Ghulam Ahmad

The Promised Messiah and Mahdi,
Founder of the Aḥmadiyya Muslim Jamā'at,
on whom be peace

ISLAM INTERNATIONAL PUBLICATIONS LTD.
TILFORD, SURREY, UNITED KINGDOM

الہدیۃ المبارکہ

یعنی کتاب

تحفۂ قیصریہ

بمقام قادیان

مطبع ضیاء الاسلام میں چھپا

۲۵ مئی سنہ ۱۸۹۷ء

Facsimile of the original Urdu title page printed in 1897.

A submission of felicitations
Namely, the book entitled

A Gift for the Queen

Published at Ḍiyāul-Islam Press, Qadian
May 25, 1897

Translation of the original Urdu title page.

A Gift for the Queen

An English rendering of *Toḥfa-e-Qaiṣariyyah,*
written by Ḥaḍrat Mirza Ghulam Ahmad,
The Promised Messiah and Mahdi, on whom be peace,
Founder of the Ahmadiyya Muslim Jama'at

Translated from Urdu into English by: Syed Sajid Ahmad
Revised by: Abdul-Wahab Mirza
Cover illustration and layout by: Salman Muhammad Sajid

First published in Urdu in Qadian, India: 1897
First English translation published in UK: 2012
(ISBN 978-1-84880-074-8)
Second revised edition published in UK: 2012
(ISBN 978-1-84880-077-9)
Third (Special) edition published in UK: 2012
Present Second edition reprinted in UK: 2018

© Islam International Publications Ltd.

Published by
Islam International Publications Ltd.
Islamabad, Sheephatch Lane
Tilford, Surrey GU10 2AQ, UK

Printed in UK at
Raqeem Press, Tilford, UK

For further information please contact:
Ahmadiyya Muslims Association UK
Baitul-Futuh, 181 London Road,
Morden, Surrey, SM4 5PT
Tel: +44 (0) 20 8687 7800
or visit www.alislam.org.

ISBN 978-1-84880-077-9
10 9 8 7 6 5 4 3 2

CONTENTS

Ḥaḍrat Mirza Ghulam Ahmad of Qadian
The Promised Messiah & Mahdi[as]

ABOUT THE AUTHOR

Ḥaḍrat Mirza Ghulam Ahmad[as] was born in 1835 in Qadian, India. From his early life, he dedicated himself to prayer, and the study of the Holy Quran as well as other scriptures. He was deeply pained to observe the plight of Islam which was being attacked from all directions. In order to defend Islam and present its teachings in their pristine purity, he wrote ninety-one books, thousands of letters, and participated in many religious debates. He argued that Islam is a living faith which can lead man to establish communion with God and achieve moral and spiritual perfection.

Ḥaḍrat Mirza Ghulam Ahmad[as] started experiencing divine dreams, visions and revelations at a young age. This communication from God continued to increase and he announced that God had appointed him to be the same Reformer of the latter days as prophesied by various religions under different titles. He also claimed to be the Promised Messiah and Mahdi whose advent had been prophesied by the Holy Prophet Muhammad (peace and blessing of Allah be upon him). In 1889, under divine command, he started accepting initiation into the Ahmadiyya

Muslim Community, which is now established in more than 200 countries.

After his demise in 1908, the institution of *khilāfat* was established to succeed him in fulfillment of the prophecy made in the Holy Quran that Allah the Almighty would establish *khilāfat* (successorship) among the Muslims. Ḥaḍrat Mirza Masroor Ahmad[aba] is the Fifth Successor to the Promised Messiah[as] and the present head of the Ahmadiyya Muslim Community.

FOREWORD

The Promised Messiah[as] wrote the book *Toḥfa-e-Qaiṣariyyah* on the occasion of the Diamond Jubilee of Her Majesty Queen Victoria. The book outlines the beautiful teachings of Islam which can establish peace and brotherhood in the world. It is also a recognition and befitting token of gratitude to the British government which provided peace and freedom of expression to all its subjects. This environment enabled the Promised Messiah[as] to propagate the message for which Allah the Almighty commissioned him. *Alḥamdolillāh*, the *Jamā'at* (Community) of the Promised Messiah[as] continues to benefit from the same peace and freedom in the UK and is engaged in serving Islam throughout the world from its headquarters in London.

If all people adhere to Quranic teachings of freedom of religion and conscience then we may establish peace and harmony in the world. May Allah guide us and help us to do so. *Āmīn*.

We are honoured to publish the English translation of the book on the auspicious occasion of the Diamond Jubilee of Her Majesty Queen Elizabeth II. All members of the *Jamā'at* are requested to read it and distribute it widely.

Please note that, in the translation that follows, words given in parenthesis ( ) are the words of the Promised Messiah[as]. If any explanatory words or phrases are added by the translator for the purpose of clarification, they are put in square brackets [ ]. Footnotes given by the Publishers are marked [Publishers]. All references, unless otherwise specified, are from the Holy Quran. Biblical references are from the King James version.

The following abbreviations have been used. Readers are urged to recite the full salutations when reading the book:

- sa *ṣallallāhu 'alaihi wa sallam*, meaning 'may the peace and blessings of Allah be upon him' is written after the name of the Holy Prophet Muhammad[sa].
- as *'alaihis salām*, meaning 'may peace be on him' is written after the name of Prophets other than the Holy Prophet Muhammad[sa].
- ra *raḍiy-Allāhu 'anhu/'anhā/'anhum*, meaning 'may Allah be pleased with him/her/them' is written after the names of the Companions of the Holy Prophet Muhammad[sa] or of the Promised Messiah[as].
- aba *ayyadahullāhu Ta'ālā binaṣrihil 'Azīz*, meaning 'may Allah the Almighty help him with his powerful support' is written after the name of the present Head of the Ahmadiyya Muslim Jamā'at, Ḥaḍrat Mirza Masroor Ahmad, Khalīfātul-Masīḥ V[aba].

This translation was prepared under the auspices and direction of Ḥaḍrat Mirza Masroor Ahmad, Khalīfatul Masīḥ V[aba]. By the grace of Allah, my humble self had the honour of working closely with Ḥuḍūr[aba] and seeking guidance and relaying his directives throughout the process of completing this translation.

I would like to express my gratitude to Syed Sajid Ahmad, who translated the book from Urdu into English, and to Mohamed Arshad Ahmedi who made the initial review. I also appreciate the assistance of Chaudhary Hamidullah Vakīl-e-A'lā and Dr. Muhammad Shafique, Deputy Vakīlut-Taṣnīf, Rabwah, Pakistan who provided assistance as and when needed. The English translation section of Additional Vakalāt-e-Taṣnīf, under the leadership of Coordinator Munawar Ahmed Saeed, carried out the revision and prepared the document for publication. The primary responsibility for revision was carried out by Abdul-Wahab Mirza with valuable assistance from Luqman Tahir Mahmood, Bilal Ahmad Rana, Fouzan Mansoor Pal and Usman Nasir Choudhary. The cover page, book layout and desktop publishing was done by Salman Muhammad Sajid. May Allah the Almighty reward them all abundantly. *Āmīn.*

Munir-ud-Din Shams
Additional Vakīlut-Taṣnīf
London, United Kingdom
April 2012

SYSTEM OF TRANSLITERATION

In transliterating Arabic words we have followed the following system adopted by the Royal Asiatic Society.

- ا at the beginning of a word, pronounced as a, i, u preceded by a very slight aspiration, like h in the English word 'honour'.
- ث *th*, pronounced like *th* in the English word '*thing*'.
- ح *ḥ*, a guttural aspirate, stronger than *h*.
- خ *kh*, pronounced like the Scotch *ch* in '*loch*'.
- ذ *dh*, pronounced like the English *th* in '*that*'.
- ص *ṣ*, strongly articulated *s*.
- ض *ḍ*, similar to the English *th* in '*this*'.
- ط *ṭ*, strongly articulated palatal *t*.
- ظ *ẓ*, strongly articulated *z*.
- ع ', a strong guttural, the pronunciation of which must be learnt by the ear.
- غ *gh*, a sound approached very nearly in the *r* '*grasseye*' in French, and in the German *r*. It requires the muscles of the

throat to be in the 'gargling' position whilst pronouncing it.

ق *q*, a deep guttural *k* sound.

ء ', a sort of catch in the voice.

Short vowels are represented by:

a for ـَـ (like *u* in '*bud*')

i for ـِـ (like *i* in '*bid*')

u for ـُـ (like *oo* in '*wood*')

Long vowels by:

ā for ـَا or آ (like *a* in '*father*');

ī for ی ـِـ or ـٖـ (like *ee* in '*deep*');

ū for و ـُـ (like *oo* in '*root*');

Other:

ai for ی ـَـ (like *i* in '*site*');

au for و ـَـ (resembling *ou* in '*sound*')

The consonants not included in the above list have the same phonetic value as in the principal languages of Europe. Curved commas are used in the system of transliteration, ' for ع, ' for ء.

We have not transliterated Arabic words which have become part of English language, e.g., Islam, Quran, Hadith, Mahdi, jihad, Ramadan, ummah, etc. The Royal Asiatic Society rules of transliteration for names of persons, places and other terms, could not be followed throughout the book as many of the names contain non-Arabic characters and carry a local transliteration and pronunciation style which in itself is also not consistent either.

INTRODUCTION

By Ḥaḍrat Maulānā Jalal-ud-Din Shams[ra]

Since the purpose of the advent of the Promised Messiah[as] was to propagate the Unity of God and His message, he found a way to serve those objectives on the occasion of the Diamond Jubilee of Queen Victoria which was celebrated with great pomp and show in June 1897. He published a book *Toḥfa-e-Qaiṣariyyah* [*A Gift for the Queen*] on May 25, 1897. In addition to felicitating Her Majesty, the Promised Messiah[as] outlined the truthfulness of the Holy Prophet[sa] and Islam with great subtlety and wisdom. He then outlined the principles which can lay the foundations of world peace and international brotherhood. After giving the gist of the Islamic teachings, he invited Her Majesty Queen Victoria to hold a conference of great religions in London so that the inhabitants of England may learn the true teachings of Islam. He then discussed the abhorrence of the Christian dogma that Ḥaḍrat 'Īsā[as] [Prophet Jesus] died on the cross and thus accepted the curse in order to save the Christians. On the joyful occasion of the Jubilee, the Promised Messiah[as] asked Her Majesty to exonerate Ḥaḍrat 'Īsā[as] [Prophet Jesus] of the curse that is wrongfully placed upon him, thereby clearing his honour from the unjustified accusation.

The Promised Messiah[as] undertook to show a sign of his own truthfulness, provided that Her Majesty would agree to accept his message in case of fulfilment—adding that he would accept the death penalty by being put on the gallows in Her Majesty's capital if he is unable to show a convincing sign.

A meeting to celebrate the Jubilee was also held in Qadian in June 1897, which was attended by several members who joined from out of town. In accordance with the directives of the government officials, a resolution was passed and sent to the Viceroy of India. Copies of *Toḥfa-e-Qaiṣariyyah* were prepared in high quality binding, one of which was sent to Deputy Commissioner District Gurdaspur for onward transmission to Her Majesty, and copies were sent to the Governor General and the Lieutenant Governor Punjab. A prayer was recited in six languages in the meeting, which included:

> Almighty God! As Thy Wisdom and Providence has been pleased to put us under the rule of our blessed Empress enabling us to lead lives of peace and prosperity, we pray to Thee that our ruler may in return be saved from all evils and dangers as Thine is the kingdom, glory and power. Believing in Thy unlimited powers we earnestly ask Thee, All-Powerful Lord, to grant us one more prayer that our benefactress the Empress, before leaving this world, may probe her way out of the darkness of man-worship with the light of *lā-ilāha illallāh Muḥammadur Rasūlullāh*. [There is no God but Allah and Muhammad is His Prophet]. Do Almighty God as we desire, and grant us this humble prayer of ours as Thy will alone governs all minds. Amen!

بسم الله الرحمٰن الرحيم
نحمده ونصلی علٰی رسوله الكريم[1]

A SUBMISSION OF FELICITATIONS

This submission of felicitations is from the person who has appeared in the name of Jesus, the Messiah, to rid the world of diverse innovations in faith. His purpose is to establish truth in the world with peace and tenderness, teach people the way of true love and obeisance to their Creator, and make them understand the ways to render true obedience to their ruler, Her Majesty the Queen, whose subjects they are. He is also to instruct mankind in true mutual sympathy and to remove selfish malice and passions among them, and establish pure harmony—unadulterated by hypocrisy—among the good natured servants of God. This writing is a gift of gratefulness, which is presented as felicitations to **Her Majesty the Empress of India and Ruler of England and India (May her honour and title endure)** at the gathering commemorating the **sixtieth jubilee**.

Felicitations! Felicitations!! Felicitations!!!

---

1. In the name of Allah, the Gracious, the Merciful. We praise Him and send blessings on His exalted Prophet[sa]. [Publishers]

Thanks to God who showed us this day of great joy that we witnessed the sixtieth jubilee of our honoured Queen, the Empress of India and England. Who can imagine the amount of joy this day has brought? Congratulations filled with joy and gratefulness from us to our benevolent and benignant Empress. May God keep her joyful forever!

We pray to God—who has created this earth and raised the heavens, and has put the radiant sun and the moon in our service—that may He keep our honoured ruler, the Empress of India, safe for a long time. She is bearing different nations of her subjects in her lap of kindness, and millions of people are living in peace because of her single person. May it be so that, at the ceremonies of the jubilee (with its ecstasy, millions of hearts from British India and England are fluttering in the excitement of joy like the flowers which, excited by the cool and comforting morning breeze, flutter their wings like birds), heaven should also felicitate her with its sun and moon and all its stars just as the earth is jumping to felicitate with all its strength! May God's grace enable our great and benevolent Empress to become as popular among the angels in heaven as she is in the hearts of all the old and young Indian and English subjects. May the Almighty, who has bestowed upon her an abundance of worldly blessings, also bestow upon her a plenitude of heavenly blessings. The Merciful, who has given her joy in this world, may He arrange for her joyful provisions in the next world too. Considering that millions, in fact countless, good deeds have been performed by such a blessed person, it would not be surprising should the providence of God cause the ultimate good to emanate from her—namely, that England may be cleared of the worship of a human being with mercy and peace, and that the souls of angels cry out, 'O true monotheist, felicitations to you from the heavens just as from the earth!'

This beseecher—who has come in the name of Jesus the Messiah—honours the person of Her Majesty, the Empress of India, and her reign; just as the Chief of this world and the next, **Holy Prophet Muhammad,** may peace and blessings of Allah be upon him, honoured the time of Nausherwan the Just. Though, keeping her favours in view, everyone is obliged to congratulate Her Majesty with sincere prayers and present a gift of gratitude to the Honoured Empress of India and England, I realize that I am more obliged than everyone else, as Allah chose for me to take refuge in the peaceful government of Her Majesty, the Queen, to carry out my heavenly activities. God raised me at such a time and in such a land where the reign of Her Majesty has the effect of a steel castle for the protection of human life and honour. It is my obligation more than anyone else to be grateful for the environment of peace in which I have lived in this land and have spread the truth. Though I have written many books in Urdu, Arabic and Persian in which I have mentioned the favours of Her Majesty on the Muslims of British India, and have spread these books in the Muslim world, encouraging every Muslim to show true obedience and fidelity, yet it was necessary for me to present the details of this activity to Her Majesty. To achieve this purpose, I have gathered the courage to fulfil the desire of my heart today on the occasion of the blessed jubilee of Her Majesty, the Empress of India, which is a source of great thankfulness and joy for the loyal subjects.

To introduce myself, I deem it necessary to state that, from among the subjects of Her Majesty, I am a member of an honoured family of the Punjab. I am known as **Mirza Ghulam**

Ahmad of Qadian. My father was Mirza Ghulam Murtaza, his father was Mirza Ata Muhammad, and his father was Mirza Gul Muhammad. The latter was a ruler in an earlier period in time. As will be described later, God took me in His service, and as He has been conversing with His people since ancient times, He honoured me, too, with His converse and communication. He established me upon utmost pristine principles which are beneficial to humanity. One of the principles upon which I have been established is the following: God has informed me that of the religions which have spread and are firmly established in the world through Prophets, holding sway over a part of the world and achieving survival and long life, none was false in its origin. Nor was any of those Prophets false, because it is the eternal practice of God that a false prophet who lies against God—who is not from God, but dares to forge things from himself—never prospers. God destroys such an audacious person who says that He is from God while God knows full well that he is not from Him. All his machinations are shattered, all of his followers are disbanded, and his future is worse than his past because he told a lie against God and brazenly maligned God. God does not give him the honour that is given to the righteous, and neither does He grant him the acceptance and stability, which is reserved for the true prophets.

The question may arise that if this is the case then why did those religions spread in the world in whose books creatures—such as humans, stones, angels, sun, moon, stars, fire, water or air, etc.—have been accepted as deities? The answer is that such religions are either from people who did not claim to be prophets and recipients of divine revelation and communication, but were inclined towards creature-worship through the falsity of their own thinking and understanding; or, there were some religions whose foundation was in fact laid by a true prophet of God but their true teachings were forgotten with the passage of time. The followers of the latter turned to creature-worship by taking some similes or parables literally. The fact is that those prophets did not teach such a religion. It is not the fault of those prophets, as they brought a wholesome and pure teaching; rather, the ignorant followers assigned perverted meaning to their statements. Such ignorant people did not claim that God's word descended on them or that they were prophets. Rather, they misunderstood and misinterpreted the prophetic word. Though such mistakes and deviations are a sin and are hateful to God, yet He does not stop their proliferation as He stops the work of a liar who lies against God. No government, whether heavenly or earthly, gives respite to a liar who fabricates a law and claims that it is authenticated by the government. A government would never allow someone to pose as a government employee and exercise authority and make people believe that he is a government official when not only is he not an officer, he is not even a lowly employee.

Therefore, this law is part of the eternal practice of Almighty God that He does not grant respite to a false prophet. Such a person is soon seized and suffers his punishment. In view of this, we shall honour and accept as true all those who claimed to be prophets at any time, and their claim was established and their religion became widespread and flourished over a long period. If we should discover mistakes in the scriptures of their religions or should observe the misconduct of their followers, we should not attribute these faults and shortcomings to the founders of these religions, inasmuch as the perversion of scriptures is possible and it is possible that mistakes of interpretation might find their way into the commentaries. But it is not at all possible that a person should fabricate lies against God and claim to be a prophet and then put forward his own compositions as the word of God falsely, and yet God should grant him respite like the righteous and allow him wide acceptance worthy of the truthful.

Therefore, this principle is an ultimate truth and endless blessing, and withal lays the foundation for conciliation, in that we affirm the truthfulness of all prophets whose religion has been well-established, has survived for a long time period and has had millions enter its fold. This is a very blessed principle. If all the world were to adhere to this fundamental principle, thousands of disorders and blasphemies, which disturb the peace among general public, would be eradicated. It is apparent that people who consider the adherents of a religion to be following a person who, in their view, is a liar and fabricator, lay the foundation of many tribulations. They certainly commit the crimes of defamation and speak of the prophets with extremely disrespectful words, going as far as employing abusive language, and disrupt harmony and peace among the general public; notwithstanding that their estimation is wrong and they are transgressors in the eyes of God with regard to their disrespectful views. God, who is Merciful and Beneficent, does not like that a liar should prosper unfairly and then put people in doubt by establishing his own religion. Nor does He allow that, in the eyes of the world, a person be raised to the level of true prophets while he is a fabricator and a liar.

Therefore, this principle lays down the foundation of love, peace and harmony, and supports moral values, in that we consider all those prophets true who appeared in the world—whether in India, or Persia or China or any other country. God instilled their respect and grandeur in the hearts of millions and made firm the roots of their religion, which remained established for centuries. This is the principle that **the Quran teaches us.** In light of this principle, we honour all religious founders who fall under this description whether they are the founders of the religion of the Hindus, or the religion of the Persians, or the religion of the Chinese, or the religion of the Jews or the religion of the Christians. Unfortunately, our adversaries cannot treat us this way, and they do not bear in mind the pristine and unalterable law of God that He does not give that blessing and honour to a false prophet that He bestows upon the true one. The religion of a false prophet does not take root and does not last long as does the religion of a truthful prophet. Therefore, people subscribing to this kind of belief—who defame the prophets of other nations by declaring them false—are always enemies of peace and harmony, because there is no greater mischief than abusing the elders of other nations. Sometimes a person would rather die than hear disparaging words for his elders. If we have an objection over the teaching of a religion, we should not attack the honour of the prophet of that religion or mention him in an unseemly manner. Rather, we should object only on the current practices of that nation. We should be certain that the prophet whom God Almighty has graced with the honour of acceptance by millions, and whose acceptance has continued for centuries, is thus firmly proven to be from Allah. If he were not the beloved of God, he would not have achieved so much respect. It is not the practice of God to grant honour to a fabricator, to spread his religion among millions, and to safeguard the fabricated religion for a long time.

Therefore, a religion which spreads in the world, takes root, and finds honour and long life, cannot at all be false in its origin. Therefore, if anything in that teaching is found objectionable, it can either be because the teachings of that prophet have been altered, or because a mistake has been made in the explanation of his teachings. It is also possible that we may not be justified in our objections. It may be observed that some priests raise objections about certain tenets in the Holy Quran, even though they believe them to be true and as the teachings of God according to the Torah. Therefore, such objections are due to one's own mistake or due to haste.

In summary, welfare of humanity, peace, harmony, righteousness, and fear of God call for adhering to the principle that we do not declare such prophets as false concerning whose truth the opinion of millions of people for centuries has been established, and they have been supported by God since time immemorial. I am confident that a seeker of truth, whether Asian or European, will cherish this principle, and will profoundly regret that he did not believe in it all along.

I place this principle before Her Majesty, the Queen, the Empress of India and England because only this principle can spread peace in the world. This is our principle. Islam is proud to be unique in subscribing to this beautiful and handsome principle. Is it befitting that we malign the sages to whom God has subjugated a world and kings have been bowing to them for centuries? Is it befitting that we be distrustful of God, thinking that He wants to deceive people by giving the status of the truthful to the liars, making them the sages of millions, giving their religions long lives and showing heavenly signs in their favour? If God Himself were to deceive us then how could we differentiate right from wrong?

This is an important tenet: a false prophet should not achieve the grandeur, acceptance and greatness as that of a truthful one. Prosperity should not result from the plans of liars as it does from the activities of a truthful one. That is why the first sign of the truthful is that perpetual support is with the truthful, and God plants his religion in the hearts of millions, and grants it long life. Therefore, keeping in view the day of our passing away and the day of recompense, we should not malign such a great sage; rather, we should garner true respect and true love for a prophet who carries such signs. This is the first principle which God has taught us. Through this we have become inheritors of a great moral code.

The second principle I have been established upon is the reformation of the wrong notion of jihad which has gained popularity among some ignorant Muslims. God the Almighty has made me understand that the ways taken as jihad these days are completely against the teachings of the Quran. No doubt, there was an order to take arms in the Holy Quran. It was more reasonable than the wars of Moses, and more acceptable than the wars of Joshua, son of Nun. It was based solely on the ground that those who unjustly raised their sword to slaughter Muslims and spilled blood unjustly and committed extreme cruelties, should also be dispatched by the sword, albeit, this punishment did not carry the severity of the wars of Moses. Rather, the punishment was waived if an Arab sought protection by accepting Islam or if a non-Arab did the same by paying *jizyah*. This procedure complied with the laws of nature. The punishments of God, which descend on the world in the form of calamities, are for sure deferred through charity, alms-giving, prayer, repentance, lowliness and humility. In the same way, when the fire of an epidemic flares greatly, all nations of the world naturally engage in prayer, repentance, seeking forgiveness and charitable giving. A natural movement takes place to turn to God, showing that it is a natural phenomenon for the human conscience to turn to God Almighty in the times of calamities. Repentance and prayer at times of calamities have proven beneficial for man, that is, a calamity is deferred through repentance and seeking forgiveness, just as the punishment of the nation of Prophet Yunus [Jonah] was deferred. In the same way, the punishment of Israelites was deferred several times through the prayers of Ḥaḍrat Moosa [Moses]. There were disbelievers who had severely persecuted Islam and Muslims, so much so that women and children were killed. God subjected them to the punishment of the sword, but then gave them reprieve due to their seeking forgiveness, repentance, and acceptance of truth. It was the same eternal way of God which has been observed throughout history.

In short, this was the root of the Islamic jihad during the time of our Prophet, may peace and blessings of Allah be upon him, that the wrath of God flared against the transgressors. But it is not jihad to plan to revolt while living under the equitable rule of a just government, such as the empire of our honoured queen Her Majesty the Empress of India; rather, it is a thinking replete with incivility and ignorance. To act maliciously towards a government which allows civic freedom, and firmly establishes peace, and under which religious rites can be fully carried out, is a criminal act rather than jihad. That is the reason why God did not appreciate the actions of the people who joined the mutiny in 1857. They faced diverse misfortunes, because they stood up against their beneficial and auspicious government. Thus, God the Almighty has established me on the principle that a beneficent government, as the British government is, be sincerely obeyed and be truly appreciated. I and my Community abide by this principle. Therefore, to assure compliance, I have written numerous books in Arabic, Persian and Urdu where I have written in detail that the Muslims of British India live comfortably under this government as they have the power to propagate their religion freely and carry out their religious obligations without hindrance. As such, how defiant and rebellious it is to entertain in our heart any thought of jihad with regard to this blessed and peace-giving government. These books were published at the expense of thousands of rupees and published in Islamic countries. I know that thousands of Muslims have been affected by these books. In particular, the people having religious affiliation with me have become truly sincere well-wishers of this government. I can claim that its parallel cannot be found among other Muslims. It is a faithful army whose life is replete with the support for the British government overtly as well as covertly.

I have also highlighted the point in my books that the objective that the ignorant mullahs want to achieve through the sword is achievable under the British government by a true religion in other ways—that is, a person can affirm his faith and refute another religion with full freedom. In my view, there is great beneficence in the Muslims having full freedom, within the limits of law, to express their religious views. Being able to attain their objective in this manner, they will do away with the militant habits which are found in some due to misunderstanding the Book of Allah. The reason for this is that, as the use of one intoxicant relieves from the use of another; similarly, when an objective can be attained one way, the other way of achieving it automatically becomes dormant.

For the same purposes, I take it as my duty to take advantage of the freedom granted by the British rule concerning religious discussions, and call upon the Islamic zealots to stop their unwarranted thoughts and inclinations. Muslim masses were waiting for a **militant messiah**, and were also waiting for a **militant mahdi.** These beliefs are so dangerous that a fabricator and liar can drown a world in blood by claiming to be the promised Mahdi, because Muslims have a tendency to this day to be ready to join any mendicant inviting to jihad. They probably cannot have such fidelity even to a king. Allah desired that such wrong thoughts be erased, and so by giving me the titles of the **Promised Messiah** and the **Promised Mahdi,** He clarified to me that waiting for a militant Mahdi or a militant Messiah is a totally wrong notion. Rather, God desires to spread the truth in the world through heavenly signs. Therefore, my principle is that the kingdoms of the world belong to the worldly kings, we do not have anything to do with their empires or wealth. The heavenly kingdom is ours. But it is necessary to also convey the message to the kings with goodly intent and true sympathy. As for this British government, since we can live peacefully under this government, it is our duty to go further and pray for its present and its future.

Alas, ever since I conveyed to the Indian Muslims that **no militant mahdi or militant messiah is to appear in the world,** and that instead a person was to come in peace **and I am that person,** the ignorant mullahs have turned against me. They consider me an infidel and outside the faith. It is surprising that these people relish the bloodshed of humans even though it is not the teaching of the Quran. Moreover, all Muslims do not hold such thoughts; it is the dishonesty of the Christian priests that they have unjustly attributed the idea of perpetual jihad to the Holy Quran. By doing so, they deceive some ignorant people and arouse their base passions. It is under divine commandment—not due to my own thoughts or volition—that I occupy myself in praying for this government under whose shadow of security I am passing my days in peace. I am grateful for its favours, and take its pleasure as my pleasure. I convey to it honestly what has been conveyed to me. Therefore, on the occasion of this jubilee—remembering the **continuous favours of Your Majesty,** which concern our lives, wealth and honour—I present **a gift of gratefulness, and that gift is the prayers** which arise from the heart and every grain of the body **for the safety and honour of Your Majesty.**

O Empress and the Honoured Queen! Our hearts bow before the Almighty praying for Your Majesty, and our souls prostrate before the One God for your honour and safety. **O Honoured Empress of India!** We congratulate you from our heart and soul on the occasion of the jubilee celebration, and pray to God that He may reward you abundantly for your beneficence that has reached us through your benign government and through your peace-loving administrators. We consider your being a great blessing from God for this land, and we regret that we cannot find words to adequately express our gratitude. May every prayer that a truly grateful one can offer for you, be accepted from us for you. May God grant you comfort with the fulfilment of your objectives. May He greatly bless your days, health and well-being. May He continue to augment your honour and glory. May He show your progeny the days of honour like yours and continue to bless them with victory and triumph. We greatly thank the Merciful and Munificent God who showed us this delightful day, and who provided us security under such a beneficent, generous, just, and intelligent queen. Under her blessed rule, she has provided us the opportunity to attain all the good of the world and of faith, so that we may carry out acts of true beneficence towards ourselves, our nation and our fellow beings, and may tread upon the path of progress freely—the path that not only saves us from the undesirable acts of the world but also enables us to attain the everlasting good of the hereafter.

When we consider all the goodness, and the means to achieve goodness, that we have gained during the reign of this Empress of India—as well as all these doors of welfare and beneficence that have opened to us during the auspicious period of her sovereignty—it provides us with strong evidence that the Empress of India harbours exceedingly good intentions for the progress of the public. It is an accepted matter that the intention of the ruler has a great effect on the internal condition, morals and behaviour of the public. Or, it can be said that when a sovereign governs over a part of land with good intentions and justice, it is the practice of God Almighty that the citizens of that land become attentive to good values and virtuous morals; and a trait of sincerity towards God and His creatures develops among them. Every eye can observe clearly that a great revolution is taking place towards good values and noble morals in British India. People with wild passions are transforming towards angelic dispositions, and the new generation has more affinity to sincerity than to hypocrisy. People's capabilities are becoming more amenable to accept the truth. A great change has occurred in the intelligence, understanding and perception of people. Most people are adopting a simpler and selfless mode of life. It appears to me that this period of rule is a harbinger of a light which is to descend from heaven to enlighten hearts. Thousands of hearts are excited in anticipation of righteousness as though they are stepping forward to welcome the heavenly guest who is the light of truth. The tinges of a positive revolution are visible in all aspects of human abilities, and the condition of hearts is becoming like a fertile land ready to bring out its greenery. Your Majesty would be justified to be proud that God **wants to initiate** a spiritual advancement **from this land** of British India. Signs of such spiritual changes are visible in this land as though God wants to pull a multitude out of lowly life. Most people are naturally inclining towards attaining a righteous life. Many souls are in search of wholesome teachings and pristine morals, and God's mercy is offering hope that they will attain their wishes.

Most people are as yet too weak to affirm the truth freely. Rather, they cannot understand truth, and the colour of prejudice is present to some extent in their writings and speeches. But it can be observed that the ability to discern truth has improved among the just people as they are now able to see the truth shine through multiple curtains.

It needs to be appreciated that a majority of people have set out in search of a heavenly light. In their eagerness to do so, some have even fallen in error and are assigning the status of the true worthy-of-worship to those unworthy of that status. Yet, there is no doubt that a movement has taken shape. The quality of discovering the reality, truth and the root of matters—and not stopping at superficial thoughts—is developing as the desirable trait. This attitude augments our hopes for the future. There is no doubt that this also results from the attitude of the ruler of the time. There is little doubt that with its entry into India, this government has ushered in an era of spiritual fervour and search for truth. No doubt it appears to be the result of the beneficence residing in the heart of our Queen, Her Majesty, concerning the public of British India.

Notwithstanding the great appreciation that I have for the benefits which have affected the physical aspects of Indian Muslims due to the attention of Her Majesty, a great portion of the beneficence of the Empress of India is that during her reign many uncivilized conditions of India are being reformed, and every person has gained a large opportunity for spiritual advancement. We see clearly that an age of true and pure reformation is drawing near and hearts continue to become attentive towards the recognition of truth. Every seeker of truth has found courage to march forward in religious matters as a result of an exchange of ideas. The True and the Only God, who was hidden from the eyes of many, seems to have determined to show His manifestations. The thought also crosses my mind that the carelessness and affluence of this land was a big hurdle in its spiritual progress and every one possessing wealth and affluence had inclined towards living well in comfort beyond moderation. If India had persisted in this condition, the present-day inhabitants of this country might have been worse than savages. Fortunately, due to the good strategy of the British government, resources of affluence and indolence have been brought under control, so that people may turn towards acquiring skills and knowledge, thereby opening the door of spiritual advancement, and reducing their inclinations towards the base passions. All these changes have taken place during the auspicious rule of Her Majesty, the Queen of India. I know quite well that misfortune and dependence are also a prescription for the promotion of human traits, provided that they remain within limits and last for a short time. Our land was in dire need of this prescription. I have personal experience in this matter. We have benefitted from this prescription much and we have acquired many spiritual jewels through it. I am from a family of the Punjab that had enjoyed the status of state-rulers during the time of the Mughal kings. Our ancestors possessed many farming villages along with the rights of sovereignty. Shortly before the rise of the Sikhs, when the ability of the Mughal kings to govern had weakened, and fiefdoms of independent states had emerged, my great grandfather, Mirza Gul Muhammad, was also a local ruler and was a sovereign in every aspect. After the Sikhs gained dominance, only eighty villages were left in his possession. Soon the zero of the number eighty also disappeared and perhaps only seven or eight villages were left. During the British rule, he was gradually left empty handed. Thus during the early time of this government, he was known to possess only five villages. My father, Mirza Ghulam Murtaza, had a chair in the court of the governor. He was such a well-wisher of the English government and brave of heart that during the 1857 uprising he supported this government beyond his means by providing fifty horses from his own resources and fifty warriors. In short, the days of our authority continued to decline and we were rendered to the condition of a minor landlord. Seemingly, this is a matter of distress as to what we used to be and what we ended up as, but when I think about it, I feel thankful to God that He saved us from many of the trials which are a sure consequence of affluence which we are seeing in this country with our own eyes. I do not want to cite specific examples of the rich and affluent which support my view. It is not befitting to present in support of my view the examples of the indolent, slothful, idle, negligent of world and faith, immersed in rich and affluent luxury, because I do not want to hurt anyone's feelings. I just want to point out here that if the authority of our ancestors had not been disturbed, we might have been immersed in the same kind of gross negligence, darkness, and base inclinations. God Almighty made the British Empire a great blessing for us, in that we were freed from hundreds of chains of this world and its mortal binds. God saved us from all the trials and tests which appear in the state of sovereignty, rule, authority and affluence; thereby destroying spiritual values. This is a grace of God that He did not want to destroy us with misfortunes and calamities that are related to a fall from authority. Rather, ridding us of insignificant sovereignty and authority in land, He bestowed on us the kingdom of heaven which is beyond the reach of the enemy. There are neither any dangers of perpetual wars and bloodshed, nor chances of machinations of enviers and misers. As He raised me in the likeness of Jesus Christ, and put the essence of Jesus in me due to the sameness in nature, it was necessary that there be a sameness with respect to a lost authority. With the loss of state, this parallel also came to be fulfilled through the will of God. Jesus was of the progeny of David, and none of the villages from the possessions of David, the king and prophet of God, were left in the possession of Jesus except for the title of prince.

I cannot exaggerate and say that I do not have a place to lay my head; but I am grateful that after all the troubles and rigours, which need not be mentioned in detail here, God Almighty took me in His lap mercifully as He had taken that blessed person whose name was **Ibrahim [Prophet Abraham].** He pulled my heart towards Him, and disclosed those matters to me which cannot be disclosed to anyone unless he enters this blessed group whom the world does not recognize because they are far removed from the world and the world is far removed from them. He disclosed to me that He is the Peerless, Unchanging, All-Powerful and Boundless God, none is like Him, and He blessed me with His communication. He directly taught me His way and informed me of all the mistakes that have entered into the beliefs of the people due to the passage of time.

He has also informed me that Jesus, the Messiah, is truly one of the very beloved and pious servants of God and is one of those who are the chosen people of God whom God purifies with His own Hand and keeps them under the shadow of His light. He is not God as has been conjectured, but has close relations with God and is among the perfect ones of which there are only a few.

Of the wonders which God has bestowed upon me, one is that I have met Jesus the Messiah several times in a state of perfect wakefulness which is called a vision. I have talked to him and have ascertained from him the nature of his real claim and teachings. A major point, which is worthy of attention, is that Jesus the Messiah is so disgusted with the doctrines of **Atonement, Trinity,** and **Sonship,** as if these are the great impostures that have been fashioned against him. This evidence of vision is not without support. I believe firmly that if a sincere seeker after truth would come and stay with me for a period and would wish to meet Ḥaḍrat Masih [the Messiah] in a vision, he would be able to do so through the blessings of my supplications and attention. He can also talk to him and receive his affirmation of what I have stated, for I am the person in whom the soul of Jesus, the Messiah, resides by way of reflection. This is a gift which is worthy of presentation to the august presence of Her Majesty, the Empress of England and India.

People of the world will not understand this matter because they lack faith in heavenly mysteries but the ones who have experienced [those mysteries] will certainly find this truth.

There are additional heavenly signs supporting my truth that are appearing through me, and the people of this country are witnessing them. My utmost desire is to transfer the certainty with which I have been blessed to the hearts of others. My desire is agitating me as how to inform Her Majesty, the Empress of India, concerning these signs. I am standing as the true ambassador from Ḥaḍrat Jesus, the Messiah. I know that what is being taught these days about Christianity is not the true teaching of Ḥaḍrat Jesus, the Messiah. I am certain that if Jesus had come in the world again, he could not even recognize these teachings.

Another great tragedy worth mentioning is that the Jews had, by their mischief and faithlessness, tried to apply the most negative application of the word 'curse' with regard to the eternally beloved, eternal sweetheart, eternally accepted of God, whose name is **Jesus.** But the Christians have also joined, to some extent, in this calumny. It has been supposed that the heart of Jesus, the Messiah, earned the application of 'curse' for three days. My body trembles with this thought and every particle of my being becomes restless. How can the word 'curse of God' be imagined to apply to the pure heart of the Messiah even for a second!!! Woe! A thousand woes, that such a belief be harboured for a beloved of God like Jesus, the Messiah, that his heart deserved the implication of the meaning of curse at any time.

I present this humble submission, not from a religious basis, but to protect the honour of a perfect human. From Jesus as his ambassador, I submit to the Empress of India that which I heard in a state of vision from his tongue. I, therefore, hope that Your Majesty will correct this wrong notion. This grave error was committed at a time when people did not ponder over the meaning of curse. But now it is the call of decency that this mistake be corrected very soon and the honour of this elite beloved of God and His chosen one be restored. In Arabic as well as in Hebrew, the word 'curse' indicates moving away from God and leaving Him. Someone is called accursed when he abandons God and becomes faithless—when he becomes the enemy of God and God becomes his enemy. That is why according to lexicon, accursed is the name of Satan, that is, the one who abandons God and is disobedient to Him. How is it possible that we propose for such a beloved of God that, God forbid, at any time, even for a second, his heart in reality abandoned God and became disobedient and rebellious to Him? How out of place is it that, to create a fictional basis for our own salvation, we put a mark of disobedience on such a beloved of God and believe that at a certain time he rebelled against and digressed from God. It is better that one should accept hell for himself than to become an enemy of the pristine honour and selfless life of such a chosen one.

Muslims claim to love Jesus, the Messiah, as much as Christians do, and his person is a common property of Christians and Muslims but I have the greatest right [to claim that love] because my nature is immersed in Jesus and his in me. Heavenly signs are appearing in support of this claim. Everyone has been invited to satisfy himself through signs about this claim if he desires to. I have gathered courage to write this much because of the true love and true respect I have for Jesus, the Messiah, in my heart—along with the statements which I heard from the tongue of Jesus, the Messiah, and the message he gave me. All these matters have moved me to become an ambassador from Jesus to the court of Your Majesty. I submit humbly that—as Your Majesty has been made protector of the lives, property and honour of millions of people, and has even issued laws for the comfort of animals and birds—how wonderful it would be that Your Majesty's attention should also turn to the **hidden disrespect** which is meted out to Jesus, the Messiah. How great would it be if Your Majesty, would research the word 'curse' through the lexicons of the world in general, and Arabic and Hebrew in particular, and take the experts' testimony of all the lexicons to ascertain that someone is called accursed only on the condition that his heart has moved away from the recognition, love and nearness of God; and rather, the enmity of God, instead of His love, has been created in his heart. That is the reason that in the Arabic lexicon accursed is the name of Satan. How can this ignoble name, that has become a part of Satan, be attributed to a pure heart? The Messiah has cleared himself from this in my vision. Common sense also dictates that the status of the Messiah is above and beyond such an allegation. The implication of curse always relates to the heart, and this is a clear matter that we cannot name a near one and a beloved of God to be cursed or accursed in any sense of the word. This is the **message** of Jesus, the Messiah, which I am delivering. It is enough proof of my truth that the signs shown at my hands are beyond human power. If Your Majesty, the Empress of India, Queen of Britain, should be interested, my God has the power to manifest a sign for Your Majesty which would be indicative of **joy and good fortune; provided that** after witnessing the sign Your Majesty would accept my message, and that effect would be given throughout the country to the mission that I hold on behalf of Jesus. But the sign to be manifested would be according to the design of God and not according to any human design. It will, however, be extraordinary and will be reflective of the Grandeur of God.[2]

Your Majesty! Please reflect with your bright cognizance, if there can be any greater disrespect in the world than to name someone renegade from God and the enemy of God, which is the implication of a curse. Therefore, how grave an insult it is that the one [Jesus] whom the angels proclaim as 'loved one of God', and who emanated from the light of God, be termed as the one distanced from God and regarded as the enemy of God!! Woe that this disrespect of Jesus is embraced by 400 million people during this age! O Honoured Queen! Do this favour to Jesus, the Messiah, and God will bless you even more. I pray that may God the Almighty inspire our beneficent Queen's heart to carry out this task. Under the influence of the Jews, during the time of Jesus, Pilate unjustly let a criminal inmate go, but not Jesus even

2. **If Your Majesty should desire to witness a sign as proof of my claim, I am certain that such a sign will be shown within one year and I will also pray that she should pass all of this period in health and security. If no sign is manifested and I prove to be false, then I am willing to be hanged in Your Majesty's capital. All this entreaty is out of my desire that our benign Queen should turn to the God of heaven, of whom the Christian faith is unaware in this age. (Author)**

though he was innocent. But, O Honoured Queen of India, we humbly submit before you that, on the occasion of the joy of the 60th jubilee, **make an effort to exonerate Jesus.** I dare to submit to you—with the purest of intentions filled with the fear of God and truth—to clear Jesus the Messiah, with courageous resolve, of this stigma placed upon his honour. No doubt, making a submission before emperors without prior permission is putting one's life on the line but at this time I accept every danger for the sake of the honour of Jesus, the Messiah, and having been called to serve as his ambassador, I stand before our just ruler. O Honoured Queen! May innumerable blessings be on you. May God relieve you of all the worries which are in your heart. Accept this representation however possible. This has been the way to resolve all religious issues from time immemorial, that when two parties differ, they first try to decide on the basis of the record available in the scriptures. When a decision cannot be reached on the basis of written evidence, they turn to reason and try to decide with rational arguments. Then, when an issue cannot be resolved with reason, they seek a heavenly decision and take the heavenly signs as the arbitrator. O Honoured Queen, all three of these sources point to the innocence of Jesus, the Messiah. From written traditions it is so, as all scriptures indicate that the heart of Jesus was humble, merciful, God-loving and was with God all the time. Why, then, is it proposed that at any time his heart, God forbid, had deviated from God, and became His denier and enemy, as the meaning of **accursed** implies. From a common sense point of view also, it does not follow that one who is a prophet and a chosen one of God—and filled with His love and whose nature is saturated with light—would, God forbid, be filled with the darkness of disbelief and disobedience; that is, darkness, which in other words is called **curse.** Furthermore, God is now giving us the news through heavenly signs that what the Quran has related about the Messiah—that he was safeguarded from the **curse** and his heart was not accursed even for a second—**is the truth.** Those signs have appeared through this humble one and are pouring like rain. Therefore, O our protector Queen, may God bless you with immeasurable bounties, **decide** this issue through your legendary just character.

I also dare to make another submission. It is evident from the historical records that when the third of the Roman Caesars ascended the throne, and had firmly established his authority, he thought of organizing a debate among the two well-known sects among the Christians, one who believed in the Oneness of God and the other that considered Jesus as god. The debate took place in the presence of the Caesar of Rome in good decorum and arrangement. Hundreds of chairs were laid to seat honoured observers and members of the government according to their status to listen to the debate. The debate of the priests from both sides lasted for forty days in the court of the king. The Roman Caesar listened to the arguments from both sides and pondered over them. In the end, the sect considering Jesus, the Messiah, to be only a messenger of God and a prophet prevailed. The other sect faced such defeat that the Caesar disclosed in the gathering that he was drawn towards the sect believing in the Oneness of God due to their argument and not of his own consideration. Before leaving the gathering, he adopted the belief of Oneness of God and became one of those mentioned also in the Holy Quran, and stopped using the phrase 'son' with reference to God.

Thereafter, the next three Caesars who ascended the throne also believed in the Oneness of God. This shows that such conferences were a tradition of the Christian kings of the past and led to great changes. Pondering over such events, it is the earnest desire of my heart that our Empress of India may also hold such a conference presided from the throne. It would be a memorable spiritual event. This conference should be of a broader scope than that held by the Caesar of Rome as our Honoured Empress has a higher status than the Roman Emperor. An additional reason for this request is that since the people of this country have come to know of the Conference of Religions in America, naturally hearts are excited that Your Majesty should also arrange such a conference in London so that, due to this event, groups of loyal subjects in this country and their leaders and scholars may meet Your Majesty at the capital; and so that Your Majesty's eyes may also fall on the thousands of loyal subjects of British India, and respected citizens of India be seen in the streets and boulevards of London for a few weeks. It will be necessary that every participant present his faith's excellences and not malign others. If such a conference takes place, it will be a legendary spiritual event from our Honoured Queen; and England, **which has been fed with Islamic matters incorrectly,** will be introduced to the true face of Islam. In this way, the people of England will be apprised of the true philosophy of every religion. It is not a satisfactory state of affairs that the information about the religions of India reaches England through priests, because the books of the priests which mention other religions are like a polluted drain of water containing much refuse and waste. The priests do not want to elicit the truth, rather they want to hide it. There is such an adulteration of prejudice in their writings that it is difficult, indeed impossible, that the real truth about religions should reach England. If they had good intentions, they would not have raised such objections on the Quran as can also be raised against the Torah of Moses. If they had fear of God, they would not have relied upon such books, which, in the view of Muslims, are unauthentic and devoid of definitive truths. Therefore, justice dictates that even if the whole of Europe were to be considered angelic, the priests would be an exception. The reason that the Christians of Europe look at Islam with hatred and dislike is that these same priests have been giving the lessons of hate by presenting unauthentic incidents. I do accept that the behaviour of some ignorant Muslims is not worthy and they have habits borne of ignorance, as some ferocious Muslims apply the term jihad to cruel bloodshed and they do not know that public's rising against a **just** ruler is mutiny and not jihad. Severance of covenant, committing evil instead of good, and murder of the innocent, whoever commits such acts should be called an offender and not a hero.

These thoughts have been produced through the perverted interpretations of the priests. There is no sign of them in the Book of God. The Word of God declares the punishment of sword for the ones who raise the sword and does not teach mutiny against the ones who establish peace, benefit the public, and give every people the rights of freedom. It is dishonesty to malign the Word of God. Therefore, it is highly desirable that for the good of humanity **a conference of religions** be held by the Empress of India to disseminate the reality of religions.

This also is worthy of submission that according to the teachings of Islam, there are only two aspects of Islamic faith. Or, we can say that this teaching consists of two main purposes. **First,** to recognize the One God as He in reality exists. To love Him and to put oneself in His true obedience as is the requirement of obedience and love. **The second purpose** is to engage all capabilities in the service and well-wishing of his people and to treat gratefully and beneficially everyone—from a king down to an ordinary person—who has done us any favour. That is why a true Muslim, who in reality is aware of his faith, always has a demeanour of sincerity and obedience towards the government under whose shadow of security he lives peacefully. The difference in religion does not hinder him from its true obedience and compliance. But the priests have completely misunderstood this matter and have surmised that Islam teaches its followers to have ill-will, enmity and a blood-thirsty attitude towards other nations. We can accept that the practical condition of some Muslims is not good and as some people of other religions commit unworthy acts by involving themselves in wrong thoughts, such people are also found among Muslims. But as I pointed out, this is not a fault of the teaching of God. Rather, it is because of the faulty attitude of those who do not ponder over the Word of God and are under the influence of their passions. In particular, the matter of jihad, which was conditional upon specific circumstances, has been misunderstood by the unwise and the ignorant so much so that they have moved far away from the Islamic teachings. Islam does not teach us at all that, being the subjects of a ruler of a foreign nation and foreign religion, and living under him in peace from every enemy, we entertain thoughts of malice and mutiny in our hearts. Rather it teaches us that if we do not thank the king under whom we live in peace then we have not even thanked God. The teaching of Islam is full of wisdom. It teaches us that a real good deed is that which fits the circumstances. God does not like mercy which does not accompany justice, and does not like justice if it does not result in assuring mercy. There is no doubt that the Quran has considered the fine points ignored by the Gospels. The teaching of the Gospel is that being slapped on one cheek, the other be presented[3] but the Quran says:[4]

جَزٰٓؤُا سَيِّئَةٍ سَيِّئَةٌ مِّثْلُهَا ۚ فَمَنْ عَفَا وَاَصْلَحَ فَاَجْرُهٗ عَلَى اللّٰهِ

In other words, the principle of justice is that the one who is injured has a right only to impart an equivalent injury. But if one forgives, provided that his forgiving is not out of place and brings about reformation, such a person will be rewarded by God. Similarly, the Gospel says, do not look at someone with desire[5] but the Quran says, do not look at the forbidden neither with desire nor without[6] because there is no better way to attain the purity of the heart.

---

3. The author refers to 'But I say unto you, That ye resist not evil: but whosoever shall smite thee on thy right cheek, turn to him the other also.' Matthew 5:39, and to 'And unto him that smiteth thee on the one cheek offer also the other; and him that taketh away thy cloak forbid not to take thy coat also.' Luke 6:29. [Publishers]
4. *Sūrah ash-Shūrā*, 42:41 [Publishers]
5. The author is referring here to 'But I say unto you, That whosoever looketh on a woman to lust after her hath committed adultery with her already in his heart.' Matthew, 5:28 [Publishers]
6. The author refers to 'Say to the believing men that they restrain their eyes and guard their private parts. That is purer for them. Surely, Allah is well aware of what they do. And say to the believing women that they restrain their eyes and guard their private parts, and that they disclose not their

The Quran is filled with similar deep wisdom and surpasses the Gospels in teaching true piety. In particular, the lamp that enables the vision of the true and unchanging God is borne only by the Quran. **If it had not come in the world** then only God knows how much the number of people who worship other created beings would have sky-rocketed. Therefore, it is a matter of gratefulness that the Oneness of God which had disappeared from the earth has been established again.

Then there is a second matter for gratefulness. God always provides firm arguments for His existence. Just as He manifested Himself to all the Prophets, and from times immemorial, illumined the world whenever He found it in the darkness, **He has not deprived the present age from His Grace**. Finding that the world had moved away from heavenly light, He determined to brighten the face of the earth with a **new light of understanding**, and to **manifest fresh signs** to illumine it.

So He sent me.

And, I am grateful to Him that He granted me a shelter under such a government that I am carrying

natural and artificial beauty except that which is apparent thereof, and that they draw their head-coverings over their bosoms, and that they disclose not their beauty save to their husbands, or to their fathers, or the fathers of their husbands or their sons or the sons of their husbands or their brothers, or the sons of their brothers, or the sons of their sisters, or their women, or what their right hands possess, or such of male attendants as have no sexual appetite, or young children who have no knowledge of the hidden parts of women. And they strike not their feet so that what they hide of their ornaments may become known. And turn ye to Allah all together, O believers, that you may succeed.' *Sūrah An-Nūr*, 24:31–32 [Publishers]

out my work of advice and guidance freely under the shadow of its kindness. Though it is incumbent on everyone of the public to be grateful to this government, I think it behooves me more than everyone else to be grateful because my sublime objectives are being accomplished under the rule of the Empress of India. Certainly, these objectives could not be accomplished under another government even if it were an Islamic government.

I do not wish to take any more of the Your Majesty's time, and so I close this submission with the following prayer.

O Powerful and Merciful Lord, keep our Honoured Queen pleased as we are pleased under the shade of her kindness. Be good to her as we are spending our lives under her beneficences, and **inspire her to graciously attend to these submissions** as only You have that power. *Āmīn*, *Āmīn* again.

Submitted by the humble one,

Mirza Ghulam Ahmad
Qadian, District Gurdaspur
The Punjab

بسم الله الرحمٰن الرحيم
نَحْمَدُهٗ وَ نُصَلِّیْ[7]

A PUBLIC MEETING OF FRIENDS

At the jubilee celebration, for prayers and gratitude for Her Majesty, the Empress of India, may she live long

I relate with great pleasure that many members of my Community travelled long distances to arrive in Qadian on June 19, 1897 to celebrate the jubilee of Her Majesty, the Empress of India, may she live long, and to express their thankfulness on that occasion. They were 225 in number. The local devotees and followers also joined them swelling the gathering greatly. They all engaged in prayer and gratitude on June 20, 1897. Proceedings were carried out nicely in accordance with the guidelines outlined in the announcement by Khan Ṣāḥib Muhammad Hayat Khan CSI, Vice President General Committee of Muslims of India. With the grace of the Almighty, the celebration was conducted accordingly: a telegram was sent from us to the Viceroy Governor General of the Indian Empire on

7. In the name of Allah, the Gracious, the Merciful. We praise Him and send blessings [on His exalted Prophet[sa].] [Publisher]

June 20, 1897 in Shimla. Then food was continuously distributed among the less affluent and needy from that day to June 22, 1897. Finally, to express our thankfulness a large feast was arranged on June 21, 1897. The less affluent and needy of the town were invited and such elaborate food was prepared as is customarily offered at weddings and was served to all present. On that day more than three hundred people participated in the feast. Illumination was arranged for the night of June 22nd. As soon as darkness set in, lamps were lit in lanes, streets, mosques and homes at every visible place. Less affluent were provided oil from personal funds. As an expression of joy, the general public was included in the feast.

This blessed gathering, for which all members donated voluntarily with great zeal, started on June 20, 1897 and continued through the evening of June 22, 1897 with great fanfare. On the first day, all members of our Community—whose names will be listed later—prayed with great sincerity for the honour and heavenly blessings for the Queen, the imperial family and the British government. All rites were carried out in accordance with the directives received in a timely fashion. Thanks to Almighty God, our Community—which includes respected government employees—prayed with great sincerity, love, complete fidelity, full zeal and delight, and showed gratefulness and contributed towards the feast for the less affluent. A large amount of voluntary contributions was also collected. They thus complied with all the directives of the General Committee so efficiently and delightfully that a better compliance cannot be imagined.

A statement, comprising prayer and gratefulness for Her Majesty, the Empress of India, was read out. Attendees cried out *Āmīn* with great enthusiasm. It was stated in six languages so that gratefulness be expressed in all the languages of the Punjab in which Muslims are well-versed. A statement in Urdu comprising gratefulness and prayer was read in the public meeting. Statements were then written in Arabic, Persian, English, Punjabi and Pushto and were read out. In Urdu because it is used in courts and is common in government offices through Imperial decree. In Arabic because it is the language of God, fountainhead of all the languages of the world, and mother of tongues from which all other languages have sprung. Moreover, the last book for the guidance of mankind, the Holy Quran, was revealed in Arabic. In Persian, because it is the legacy of the former Muslim kings who ruled this country for about seven hundred years. In English, as it is the language of Her Majesty, the Queen, the Empress of India, and its respected members, to whom we are grateful for their justice and beneficence. In Punjabi, as it is our mother tongue in which it is imperative to express our gratitude. In Pushto, as it is a link between our mother tongue and the Persian language and represents the glory of our frontier.

On the occasion of this celebration, a book was compiled in gratefulness for the Empress of India and was published with the title of *Toḥfa-e-Qaiṣariyyah* [*A Gift for the Queen*]. A few copies were very beautifully bound. One copy was sent to the Deputy Commissioner for onward submission to the Empress of India, and another was sent to respected Viceroy Governor General, Indian region. One copy was sent to Nawab Lieutenant Governor of the Punjab. We write below the prayers which were offered in six languages followed by the names of all the friends who travelled to Qadian for this public meeting. In intense hot weather, they bore the hardship cheerfully and many happily slept on the ground for three days, as enough cots could not be provided due to the large attendance. I do not find words to express the sincerity, love and fidelity of heart with which the honoured members of my Community celebrated this rite of joy.

I missed mentioning earlier that during the course of the public meeting, on June 22, 1897, four of our scholars stood up to exhort the general public for the obedience and true fidelity to the Empress of India. First, our brother Maulavī Abdul Karim stood up and spoke on the matter. Then our brother Ḥaḍrat Maulavī Ḥakīm Nūr-ud-Dīn Bheravī made a speech. After him, our brother Maulavī Burhan-ud-Din Jhelumi got up and spoke in Punjabi encouraging the general public to obey Her Majesty, the Queen. After him, Maulavī Jamal-ud-Din of Syedwala, District Montgomery, stood up and spoke in Punjabi. He focused on the point that Ḥaḍrat Masih [Jesus], peace be on him, for whom uninformed Muslims are still awaiting in a militant role, has in reality passed away. The idea that Muslims at some time, on the coming of the Mahdi and Messiah, will engage in blood-shedding is not true. He admonished the general public to adopt good conduct and righteousness. At this blessed instance, sixty to seventy men repented form all sin and misconduct, crying so much so that the mosque was resounding with their weeping and wailing.

The prayers offered in six languages mentioned are given below.

Writer,

Mirza Ghulam Ahmad of Qadian
June 23, 1897

PRAYER IN URDU

دعا اور آمین اردو زبان میں

اے مخلصان باصدق وصفا ومحبّان بے ریا جس امر کے لئے آپ سب صاحبان تکلیف فرما ہوکر اس عاجز کے پاس قادیان میں پہنچے ہیں وہ یہ ہے کہ ہم جناب ملکہ معظّمہ قیصرہ ہند کے احسانات کو یاد کر کے ان کی سلطنت دراز شصت سالہ کے پوری ہونے پر اس خدائے عزّوجل کا شکر کریں جس نے محض لطف واحسان سے ایک لمبے زمانہ تک ایسی ملکہ محسنہ کے زیر سایہ ہمیں ہر ایک طرح کے امن سے رکھا۔ جس سے ہماری جان و مال وآبرو جابروں اور ظالموں کے حملہ سے امن میں رہی۔ اور ہم تمام تر آزادی سے خوشی اور راحت کے ساتھ زندگی بسر کرتے رہے۔ اور نیز اس وقت ہمیں بغرض ادائے فرض شکرگذاری جناب ملکہ معظّمہ قیصرہ ہند کے لئے جناب الٰہی میں دعا کرنی چاہیئے کہ جس طرح ہم نے ان کی سلطنت میں امن پایا اور ان کے زیر سایہ رہ کر ہر ایک شریر کی شرارت سے محفوظ رہے اسی طرح خدا تعالیٰ جناب ممدوحہ کو بھی جزاءِ خیر بخشے۔ اور ان کو ہر ایک بلا اور صدمہ سے محفوظ رکھے اور اقبال اور کامیابی میں ترقیات عطا فرمائے اور ان سب مرادوں اور اقبالوں اور خوشیوں کے ساتھ ایسا فضل کرے کہ انسان پرستی سے ان کے دل کو چھڑا دیوے۔ اے دوستو! کیا تم خدا کی قدرت سے تعجب کرتے ہو اور کیا تم اس بات کو بعید سمجھتے ہو کہ ہماری ملکہ معظّمہ قیصرہ ہند کے دین اور دنیا دونوں پر خدا کا فضل ہو جائے۔ اے عزیزو! اس ذات قادر مطلق کی عظمتوں پر کامل

ایمان لاؤ جس نے وسیع آسمانوں کو بنایا اور زمین کو ہمارے لئے بچھایا اور دو چمکتے ہوئے چراغ ہمارے آگے رکھ دیئے جو آفتاب اور ماہتاب ہے۔ سو سچے دل سے حضرت احدیت میں اپنی محسنہ ملکہ قیصرہ ہند کے دین اور دنیا دونوں کے لئے دعا کرو۔ میں سچ سچ کہتا ہوں کہ جب تم سچے دل سے اور روح کے جوش کے ساتھ اور پوری امید کے ساتھ دعا کرو گے تو خدا تمہاری سنے گا۔ سو ہم دعا کرتے ہیں اور تم آمین کہو کہ اے قادر توانا جس نے اپنی حکمت اور مصلحت سے اس محسنہ ملکہ کے زیر سایہ ایک لمبا حصہ ہماری زندگی کا بسر کرایا اور اس کے ذریعہ سے ہمیں صدہا آفتوں سے بچایا اس کو بھی آفتوں سے بچا کہ تو ہر چیز پر قادر ہے۔ اے قادر توانا! جیسا کہ ہم اس کے زیر سایہ رہ کر کئی صدموں سے بچائے گئے اس کو بھی صدمات سے بچا کہ سچی بادشاہی اور قدرت اور حکومت تیری ہی ہے۔ اے قادر توانا ہم تیری بے انتہا قدرت پر نظر کر کے ایک اور دعا کے لئے تیری جناب میں جرأت کرتے ہیں کہ ہماری محسنہ قیصرہ ہند کو مخلوق پرستی کی تاریکی سے چھڑا کر لا الہ الا اللہ محمد رسول اللہ پر اس کا خاتمہ کر۔ اے عجیب قدرتوں والے! اے عمیق تصرفوں والے! ایسا ہی کر۔ یا الٰہی یہ تمام دعائیں قبول فرما۔ تمام جماعت کہے کہ آمین۔ اے دوستو اے پیارو۔ خدا کی جناب بڑی قدرتوں والی جناب ہے۔ دعا کے وقت اس سے نومید مت ہو کیونکہ اس ذات میں بے انتہا قدرتیں ہیں اور مخلوق کے ظاہر اور باطن پر اسکے عجیب تصرف ہیں سو تم نہ منافقوں کی طرح بلکہ سچے دل سے یہ دعائیں کرو۔ کیا تم سمجھتے ہو کہ بادشاہوں کے دل خدا کے تصرف سے باہر ہیں؟ نہیں بلکہ ہر ایک امر اس کے ارادہ کے تابع اور اس کے ہاتھ کے نیچے ہے۔ سو تم اپنی محسنہ قیصرہ ہند کیلئے سچے دل سے دنیا کے آرام بھی چاہو اور عاقبت کے آرام بھی۔ اگر وفادار ہو تو راتوں کو اٹھ کر دعائیں کرو۔ اور صبح کو اٹھ کر دعائیں کرو۔ اور جو لوگ اس بات کے مخالف ہوں انکی پرواہ نہ کرو۔ چاہیئے کہ ہر ایک بات

تمہاری صدق اور صفائی سے ہو اور کسی بات میں نفاق کی آمیزش نہ ہو۔ تقویٰ اور راستبازی اختیار کرو۔ اور بھلائی کرنے والوں سے سچے دل سے بھلائی چاہو تا تمہیں خدا بدلہ دے کیونکہ انسان کو ہر ایک نیکی کے کام کا نیک بدلہ ملے گا۔

اب زیادہ الفاظ جمع کرنے کی ضرورت نہیں۔ یہی دعا ہے کہ خدا ہماری یہ دعائیں سنے۔ والسلام

PRAYER IN ARABIC

الدّعَاءُ والتّامين فى العَرَبيّة

ايّها الاحبّاء المخلصون. والاصدقاء المسترشدون. جزاكم اللّٰه خير الجزاء. وحفظكم فى الكونين من البلاء. انكم قاسيتم متاعب السّفر و شوائبه. و ذُقتم شدائد الحرّ ونوائبه. وجئتمونى مُدلجين مدّلجين مُكابدين. لتشكروا اللّٰه فى مكانى هٰذا مجتمعين. وتكثروا الدّعاء لقيصرة الهند شاكرين ذاكرين. وتدعون دعوة المخلصين. ياعباد اللّٰه لا تعجبوا لدعواتنا وشكرنا فى تقريب الجوبلى. وتعلمون ماقال سيدّنا امام كل نبىّ وولى ـ وخاتم النبيّين . انه مَنْ لم يشكر الناس فما شكر اللّٰه وَ اللّٰه يحبّ المحسنين. ثمّ تعلمون انّ اموالنا واعراضنا ودماء نا قد حفظتها العناية الالٰهيّة بهٰذه الملكة المعظمة. وجعلها اللّٰه مؤيّدة لنا فى المهمّات الدنيويّة والدّينيّة. فالشكر واجب علىٰ مافعل ربّنا ذوالجلال والعزة ومن اعرض فقد كفر بالنعم الرحمانية. واللّٰه يحبّ الشاكرين. ايّها النّاس هذا يوم يجب فيه اظهار الشكر والمسرّة مع الدّعاء باخلاص النيّة. فاردنا اَنْ نقبله بمراسم التهانى والتبريک والتهنيّة. ورفع اكفّ الابتهال والضراعة. وتذلّل يليق بحضرة الاحدية. وانارة الماٰذن والمساجد والسكک والبيوت

بالمصابيح والشهب النورانيّة. وانما الاعمال بالنيات المخفية من اعين العامة. واللّٰه يرى مافى قلوب العالمين. ياعباد اللّٰه الرحمان. هل جزاء الاحسان الّا الاحسان. فلا تظنواظنّ السوء. مستعجلين والأن ادعوا لقيصرة بخلوص النيّة. فامّنو علٰى دعائى يامعشر الاحبّة. واتّقوا اللّٰه ولا تنسوا منّ اللّٰه و منّ عباده من الخواص والعامة. ولا تعثوا مفسدين.

يا ربّ اَحسِنُ الٰى هٰذه الملكة. كما احسنت الينا بانواع العطيّة. واحفظها مِن شرّ الظالمين. ياربّ شيّد واعضد دعائم سريرها. واجعلها فائزة فى مهمّاتها وصُنها من نوائب الدنيا وآفاتها. وبارك فى عمرها و حياتها ياا رحم الراحمين. ياربّ ادخل الايمان فى جذر قلبها ونجّها و ذراريها مِن ان يعبدوا المسيح ويكونوا من المشركين. ياربّ لا تتوفّها الّا بعد ان تكون من المسلمين. ياربّ انا ندعو لها بأَلسنة صادقة وقلوب ملئت اخلاصا وحسن طويّة فاستجب يااَحُكم الحاكمين.

اجد الانام ببهجة مستكثره	عيد اتٰى او جوبلى القيصرة
نشر التهانى فى المحافل كلها	فارى الوجوه تهللت مُستبشره
انّى اراها نعمةً من رَبّنا	فالشكر حق واجب لا بربره
لا شك ان سرورنا من شكرها	خير فمن يعمله اخلاصًا يره
اَمَرَ النّبىُّ لشكر رجل محسن	قُتل العنود المعتدى ما اكفره

PRAYER IN PERSIAN

دُعاو آمین در زبانِ فارسی

اے گروہ دوستان و جماعت مخلصان خدا شمارا اجزاءِ خیر دہد شما تکالیف گرمی موسم و صعوبت سفر برداشتہ نزد من در قادیان بدین غرض رسیدہ اید کہ تا بر تقریب جشن جوبلی باجتماع اخوان خود شکر خدائے عزّ وجل بجا آرید و برائے خیر دُنیا و دین ملکہ معظّمہ قیصرہ ہند دعاہا کنید ۔ می دانم کہ موجب ایں تکالیف و آنچہ برائے انعقاد ایں جلسہ باہم چندہ فراہم کردہ رسوم جلسہ بجا آوردہ اید باعث ایں ہمہ بجز اخلاص و محبّت چیزے دیگر نبودہ ۔ پس دعا می کنم کہ خُدا تعالےٰ شمارا پاداش ایں تکالیف دہد کہ محض برائے حصول مرضات او کشیدہ اید ۔ اے دوستان می دانید کہ ما در عہد سعادت مہد قیصرہ ہند چہ آرامہا دیدیم و می بینیم و چہ قدر زندگی خود در امن و عافیت گذرانیدہ ایم و می گذرانیم ۔ پس شرط انصاف این است کہ ما برائے ایں ملکہ مبارکہ از تہ دل دُعا کنیم چرا کہ ہر کہ شکر مردم محسن نہ کند شکر خدا بجا نیاوردہ است ۔ پس ایں دعاہا میکنم شما آمین بگوئید ۔ اے قادر توانا بدیں ملکہ تو نیکی کُن چنانکہ او بما کرد ۔ و از شر ظالمان او را محفوظ دار ۔ اے قادر توانا ستونہائے سریر او بلند کُن و در مہمات خود او را فائز گردان واز حوادث دُنیا و دین اُورا نگہ دار ۔ و در عمر و زندگی او برکت بخش ۔ اے قادر توانا اسلام در دِل اُو داخل کُن و اُورا و اولاد اُو را از پرستش مسیح کہ بندۂ عاجز است نجات دِہ واز مشرکان او را بیرون آر کہ ہمہ قدرت تو داری ۔ اے قادر توانا او را تا آن وقت وفات مدہ کہ بر راہِ راست اسلام ثابت قدم بودہ باشد ۔ اے ربّ جلیل دعاہائے ما قبول کُن ۔ آمین ۔

PRAYER IN PUSHTO

دُعَا نورُ آمِیُن پُو پَشُتو ژبَه کِرُ

اَیُ دمابُلُ دِخُدای دُوستُونُ خُداتا سِتَه دِ خَیُر جَزا درُ کِرے تاسِه
خَلُق تگلیُفَون پُخُپُلُ زَان بَانِد آخِسُتی دَهُ دِمَا ححه پوُ قَادِیَان لِپاره دِ
دِغَرَضُ رَاغلِے وُه کِه دِ مَلِکهُ مُعظّمه اِشُپے تِرُ کالُ جَشُن اِسُتَاسُو اوُرُوُ
رُوُن سَرَهُ دِرُ خُدائے عزَوَجَلّ شُکرَ اَدا وُکروُاَوُر دِرے مَلِکهُ معظّمه
قَیُصره هِنُد دُنُیائی خَیُر لِپَارَهُ دُعا وکُوز پوُئے گمُ کِه دِدِ تکلیفونَ سَبَبُ
چه جَلسَهُ دِپَارَهُ چِنُدَه توله کَرَ ے وُه بُلُ دِجَلسَه رَسُم بَهَمُ پُوُرَهُ کَرَ ے
وُه دِ اِخُلاص اَود دِرُ حُجَتُ سِوا بُل شِرُ نِدَرُ نورُ زِ دُعاکَوُمُ کِهُ خُدا
صاحِبُ تاسُتَه دِدِ تکلیفونَ اَجر وَرُکِي چه صرُف دِ آغَهُ لِپَارَهُ تاسوُ
آخِسُتَیُ دَه . اَے دوسُتونَ پویُگیُ چه مُنگهُ دِ مَلِکه کِرے پوُ زمَانِے مِیُن
سِرِنُکهُ آرام مُنُگهٗ لِیُدِلَےُ دَهُ اَوُزَه سِرِنگهٗ دِخپُلُ زِنِدگی سَرَهُ بَسَرُ کَرِیُ
هَمُ دَهُ اَوُر بَسَرُبَه اوکُو بُیا اِنُصَافُ دَادَهُ چِهُ مُنکهٗ دِ مَلِکَهُ دِ پارَهُ دُعا وَکُو
وَلِے چه هَرُچَاچه دِ نیک سَرَیُ شُکرنَکیُ اَغَهُ دِ خُدای شُکر سِرِنَگه
کَوُلےُ شِیُ. پَسُ زِ دُعَا کَوُمُ تَاسِهُ آمِیُن وَه وَائی اےُ لوُئے خُدایا دِ مَلِکَهُ
سَرَهُ نِیکیُ وُه کَهُ اَغَهُ سِرُ چه مُنَکهٗ سَرِهُ اَغَهُ کَر ے دِرے اَوُر دِ ظالمون
دِشَرَه اَغه اُوسَاتَه یالوئے خُدایَادِ اَغه دِ تَخُت اِسُتِنِ تهُ بِلُنُد

اُوکره بُل دَدین اَورُدَ دنیا شِرُونَ اَغه اُوسَاتَه اَوُر پوُعُمُر بُلُ پُو اغَهَ زِنُدگی بَرَکَتُ کَرَهُ یا لوئِے خُدَایَا اِسُلَامُ پوُ اَغَه زِرَهُ بُنَهُ کَره یا لویُ خُدایا مَلِگَهُ بُلُ دِ اَغه زویُ بُلُ دِ اَغَهَ عَیَال دِیُ مَسِیحُ دیُ پَرسُتش چه یَوُ عَاجِزُ سَرَ یُ دَه اوسَاتَه اَوردِ مُشرِکُونَ دِگرُوهُنَه اَغَه اوباسَهُ چه تَه قُدرَتُ لَرَیُ اَیُ لوئِے خُدایَا تِرُاَغَه وقُت مَلِگه مُرمُکَهُ چه مُسُلمَان شِیُ یالوئِے خَدایَا اِمنگ دُعَاته قبَول کَرَه.

PRAYER IN PUNJABI

مہارانی قیصرہ ہند دیاں ساریاں مُراداں پوریاں ہوندی پنجابی وِچہ بینتی

سُنو میریو سچے دوستو تے پکے یارو جس گل واسطے تُسیں سارے بھائی اپنے سارے کم کُسا کے تے کشالہ کر کے میرے کول قادیان وچہ آئے او اوہ اک بھارا متبل ایہ ئے جے اسیں سارے دربار رانی ملکہ معظّمہ قیصرہ ہند دیاں احساناں تے مہربانیاں نوں یاد کر کے اوہدے سٹھ ورھیاں دے راج دے پورا ہونے دی اپنے ربّ دے درگاہے شکر کریئے تے ایس دے بے اوڑک کرم دا گاون گایئے جس نے آپنیاں فضلاں تے کرماں دے نال ایڈے لمّے زمانے توڑیں سانوں اجیہی ملکہ معظّمہ دے راج دے چھاویں بھاگاں سہاگاں نال رکھیا۔ جس تھیں اساں غریباں مسلماناں دیاں جاناں تے پُتاں تے مال ہتھیاریاں تے انیائیاں دے پنجیاں تھیں بچ گئے تے اسیں ہُن توڑیں من بھاوندیاں خوشیاں تے انگنیاں چیناں دے نال اپنی زندگانی پوری کر دے رہے۔ تے دوجا متبل وڈا ایہ جے ہن اسیں اس ویلے جناب ملکہ معظّمہ دا شکر پورا کرنے واسطے سچّے رب صاحب دی سچّی درگاہے ترلیاں تے جھیر گیان نال دعا کریئے کہ جس طرح ایس جگت دی رانی تے دھرمی تے لاڈلڈیانے والی ماتا دے راج وچہ رہ کے اساں آرام پایا تے اوس دی بادشاہی دی ٹھنڈی تے سنگھنی چھاں وچ ہر انرتھی دے انرتھوں بچکے مٹھّیاں نیندراں سُتّے ہاں اوسےّ طرح دھرتی انبر دا راجا سچّا ربّ ایسی ملکہ معظّمہ نوں اینہاں پُتّاں دا نانند ابدلہ دے۔ تے اوہنو ہر اک تھکے تھوڑے تے ساریاں درداں تھیں آپنا ہتھ دے کے بچار کھے۔ تے اقبال تے وڈیائی تے آساں امیداں دے پورا ہوون وِچہ وادھا بخشے تے ساریاں مُراداں پوریاں کرنے

سمیت اوستے ایسا فضل کرے تے اجیہا ترٹھے جے بندہ پرستی تھیں اوسدے دِل نوں مٹھی نیندروں جگاوے تا ایہ ماتا آپنی جاؤ واسمیت اک وحدہٗ لاشریک لہٗ جیوندے جاگدے دھرتی انبر تے ایس سارے اڈنبر دے سائیں دی پوجا ول آوے۔ تے دوہاں جگاں دا سدا سرگ پاوے۔ میریو پیاریو یارو تسیں خدا دی قدرت تھیں اوپرا جاندے ہو۔ بھلا تسیں ایسی گل نوں اچرج تے انہونی سمجھدے ہو جے ساڈی جگ رانی ملکہ معظّمہ دے دین تے دُنیاں تے خدا دا فضل ہو جائے۔ او پیاریو اُس ذات سکت واندیاں وڈیائیاں تے پُورا ایمان لیاؤ جس نے ایڈا چوڑا تے اُچّا آسمان بنایا تے دھرتی نوں ساڈے واسطے وچھایا تے دو چمکدے دیوے انملے جگ چمکان والے ساڈیاں اکھیاں اگے رکھے۔ اک چندر ماہ دوجا سورج ماہ سوتر لیاں تے ہاڑیاں تے دندیاں لہلکنے نال ربّ صاحب سچّے دی درگاہ وچہ اپنے سَد اُپنّاں داناں والی ملکہ معظّمہ دے دین تے دُنیاں واسطے دُعا منگو۔

میں سچّو سچ کہناہاں جیکر تُسیں کچیاں تے دو۲ گلّیاں نوں سنگوں ہٹا کے تے سچّیاں تے اکولّیاں نوں ساتھ لے کے تے پوری امید نال نہچہ بنہ کے دُعا کروگے تاں جگاں دا سچّا داتا تہاڈی دُعا ضرور سُنے گا۔ سو اسیں دُعا کرنے ہاں تے تسیں آمین آکھو۔ ہے سچّیا سکتاں والیا سچیا سائیاں جدتوں آپنی حکمت تے مصلحت نال ایس دیاوان رانی دے راج دے ٹھنڈی چھاویں ساڈے جیونیدا اک لمّا حصّہ پورا کیتائی تے اوس دے سبّبوں ہزاراں آفتاں تے بلاواں تھیں سانوں بچایائی۔ تُوں اُسنو بھی آفتاں تھیں بچا جے توں ہر شَے تے سکت تے وس رکھنائیں۔ ہے قدرتاں والیاں جس طرح اسیں اوسدے راج وچہ دھکیاں دھوڑیاں تے ٹھینے ڈگنے تھیں بچائے گئے ہاں اوسنوں بھی ساریاں چنتاں تے چھوریاں تھیں بچا جے سچّی بادشاہی تے پکّی زورآوری تے پوری حکومت تیری ہیئے۔ ہے جتناں والیا مالکا اسیں تیری بے انت قدرت تے تہان رکھ کے اک ہور دُعا دے واسطے تیری درگاہے دلیری کرنے ہاں جے توں ساڈی اَن گنت دَیاوان رانی ملکہ معظّمہ نوں بندہ پوجن دی انہیری کوٹھڑی تھیں باہر کڈھ کے اُچّے تے سنہری تے لاٹاں مارنے والے لا الٰہ اِلّا اللّٰہ محمّد رسول اللّٰہ دے چبوترے تے موجاں ماننے والی کر کے اوسے تے اوہدا پورن کر۔ ہے اچرج زورانوالیا۔ ہے ڈوھنگیاں نگاہاں والیا۔ ہے

پوریاں پہچان والیا۔ ہے بے اوڑک کا بواں والیا اینویں کر۔ ہے ربّاں دیا ربّا ایہ ساریاں دُعاواں منظور کر۔ سارے دوست آمین آکھو۔ اے پیاریو سچے ربدی درگاہ وَڈِی قدرتاں تے پہنیاں والی درگاہ ئے دعا دے ویلے اوس تھیں بے امید نہ ہووو۔ کیوں جے اوس دے دربار دے بے اوڑ سدا درتوں کسے سمے کوئی پھکھارا پھکھاتے خالی ہتھ نہیں گیا۔ تے اپنے سربت جیا جنت دے اندر باہراوہدے اچرج کابو تے قبضے ہین۔ تسیں دوگلیاں تے دورنگیاں تے کھوٹیاں وانگر دعا نہ کرو۔ سگوں سچیاں چیلیاں تے سوچیاں چیریاں وانگوں اوہدے من دھن تے چت ست تے پت واسطے دھن شاوا کھوتے سدا سُکھ منگو۔ ہین تسین سمجھدے ہو جے سربت راجیاندے دِل اُس مہاراج سرب شکتی مان سدا دیاوان دے کابوؤں باہر نہیں سگوں سارے کم تے انیک تے ان گنی کرتب اُسیدے اوڈاؤ ہتھ وچہ نے۔ سوتسیں اپنے ان گنت دانا نوالی مہارانی ملکہ معظّمہ دے دُنیا تے عاقبت واسطے آنند تے آرام منگو جے تسیں وفادار ٹھیلیے تے مَن وارنے والے چاکر ہوتاں شامیں تے پھرراتیں تے پچھلی راتیں نیندراں گنوا کے اوبھڑ وائی اُٹھ اُٹھ کے بینتیاں کرو تے جھڑے مُنکھ اس گلدے دوتی تے دوکھی ہون اُنہاں ہتھ یاریاندی پرواہ نہ کرو۔

لوڑیدائی جے سبھّو گلاّں تہاڈیاں نتریاں ہوئیاں تے سُتھریاں ہون تے کسے گل تھہاڈّی وچہ رلا رول نہ ہووے سُرت تے سچ ملّو بھلا کرن والیاں دا بھلا چاہوتاں تھہانوں تھہاڈا جانی جان سچّا رب صاحب چنگا بدلہ دیوے۔ کیوں جے ہرمنکھ بے حیائی کپدائی تے کیتائی پاندائے۔ نریاں گلاں کجھ پھل نہیں دیندیاں۔ تھڑیاں تے تھڑیاں نوں پکڑنے والیا بھوؤ ڑیداویلائی۔

PRAYER
IN ENGLISH

English Translation of the prayer recited by Mirza Ghulam Ahmad, Ra'īs of Qadian, on the Occasion of the Diamond Jubilee [of Her Majesty Queen Victoria.]

My friends - The object which has brought you here is to convene a meeting of thanksgiving on the happy occasion of the Diamond Jubilee of Her Majesty's reign in remembrance of the manifold blessings enjoyed by us during Her Majesty's time. We offer our heartfelt thanks to God who out of His special kindness has been pleased to place us under this sovereign rule, protecting thereby our life, property and honour from the hands of tyranny and persecution and enabling us to live a life of peace and freedom. We have also to tender our thanks to our gracious Empress, and this we do by our prayers for Her Majesty's welfare. May God protect our beneficent sovereign from all evils and hardships as Her Majesty's rule has protected us from the mischief of evil doers. May our blessed ruler be graced with glory and success and be saved at the same time from the evil consequences of believing in the divinity of a man and his worship. My friends do not wonder at this, nor entertain any doubt as to the wonderful powers of the Almighty, because it is quite possible for Him to confer His choicest blessings upon our gracious Queen in this world and the next. Hence a strong and firm belief in the Omnipotence of the Supreme Being who made this spacious firmament on high and spread the earth beneath our feet illuminating them both with the sun and the moon. Let your sincere prayers as to the good of Her Majesty in matters spiritual and temporal, reach His holy throne. And I assure you that prayers that come from hearts sincere earnest and hopeful are sure to be listened to. Let me pray then and you may say Amen:

Almighty God! As Thy Wisdom and Providence has been pleased to put us under the rule of our blessed Empress enabling us to lead lives of peace and prosperity, we pray to Thee that our ruler may in return be saved from all evils and dangers as Thine is the kingdom, glory and power. Believing in Thy unlimited powers we earnestly ask Thee, All-Powerful Lord, to grant us one more prayer that our benefactress the Empress, before leaving this world, may probe her way out of the darkness of man-worship with the light of *lā-ilāha illallāh Muḥammadur Rasūlullāh*. [There is no God but Allah and Muhammad is His Prophet]. Do Almighty God as we desire, and grant us this humble prayer of ours as Thy will alone governs all minds. Amen!

My Friends! Trust in God and feel not hopeless. Do not even imagine that the minds of worldly potentates and earthly kings are beyond His control. Nay, they are all subservient to His Holy Will. Let therefore your prayers for the welfare of your Empress in this world and the next, come from the bottom of your hearts. If you are loyal subjects, remember Her Majesty in your night and morning prayers. Pay no heed to opposition. Let Your words and deeds be true and free from hypocrisy. Lead lives of virtue and righteousness, and pray for the good of your well-wishers, because no virtue goes unrewarded. I conclude with earnest desire that God may grant our prayer. Amen.

[Dated: 23-6-1897]

MEETING ATTENDEES

Names of the attendees at the public meeting to celebrate the Diamond Jubilee in Qadian, District Gurdaspur, with our Imam the Promised Messiah and Imam Mahdi. With contribution or without, and the names of the absentees who contributed. From June 20, 1897 to June 22, 1897.

№	NAME	RESIDENCE	DONATED	COMMENTS
1	Ḥaḍrat Mirza Ghulam Ahmad, the Promised Messiah and Imām Mahdī, Chief of Qadian, with family	Qadian	Rs. 51	
2	Ḥaḍrat Maulavī Ḥakīm Nūr-ud-Dīn Bheravī	"	Rs. 5	
3	Maulavī Abdul Karim	Sialkot	Rs. 3	
4	Maulavī Burhan-ud-Din	Jhelum	½ anna	
5	Maulavī Muhammad Ahsan	Amroha Distt. Moradabad	Rs. 3	could not be present due to constraints
6	Hakeem Fazl-ud-Din with two families	Bhera	Rs. 10	
7	Khawaja Kamal-ud-Din, B.A. Professor Islamiyyah College	Lahore	Rs. 5	

№	NAME	RESIDENCE	DONATED	COMMENTS
8	Mufti Muhammad Ṣādiq Bheravi—Clerk Accountant General	Lahore	Rs. 2	
9	Mirza Ayub Beig—BA-student in Lahore, with family	Kalanaur	Rs. 2	
10	Khalifah Rajb-ud-Din—Rice Trader	Lahore	Rs. 4 & 12 annas	
11	Hakeem Muhammad Husain	〃	Rs. 1	
12	Khawaja Jamal-ud-Din—B.A., Ranbir College, Jammu State	〃	Rs. 2	
13	Hakeem Fazl Ilahi	〃	Rs. 5	
14	Munshi Maula Bakhsh—Clerk railway offices	〃	Rs. 1	
15	Munshi Nabi Bakhsh—〃	〃	Rs. 3	
16	Munshi Muhammad Ali 〃	〃	Rs. 1	
17	Munshi Muhammad Ali—M.A., Professor Oriental College	〃	Rs. 5	
18	Sheikh Rahmatullah—Garment Trader	〃	Rs. 25	
19	Munshi Karam Ilahi—Administrator Madrasah Nusrat-e-Islam	〃	4 annas	
20	Miań Muhammad Azeem—Clerk Railway Offices	Lahore	8 annas	
21	Ḥāfiẓ Fazl Ahmad with son	〃	Rs. 1	
22	Ḥāfiẓ Ali Ahmad 〃	〃	Rs. 1	

№	NAME	RESIDENCE	DONATED	COMMENTS
23	Sheikh Abdullah—new Muslim, Administrator Anjuman Himayat-e-Islam Hospital	〃	8 annas	
24	Ali Muhammad—BA-student	〃	½ anna	
25	Munshi Abdur Rahman—Clerk Railway Offices	〃	Rs. 5	
26	Munshi Miraj-ud-Din—General Contractor	Lahore	8 annas	
27	Munshi Taj-ud-Din—Clerk Railway Offices	〃	Rs. 1	
28	Sheikh Din Muhammad	〃	8 annas	
29	Hakeem Sheikh Nur Muhammad—new Muslim	〃	Rs. 1	
30	Hakeem Muhammad Husain—Proprietor, Rafiqus-Ṣiḥat Factory	〃	Rs. 1	
31	Taj-ud-Din—Student Madrasah Islamiyyah	〃	½ anna	
32	Abdullah—〃	〃	½ anna	
33	Maula Bakhsh Patauli	〃	Rs. 1	could not be present due to constraints
34	Qazi Ghulam Husain Bheravi—Art School-Student	〃	8 annas	〃
35	Haji Shahab-ud-Din	〃	Rs. 4	〃
36	Charagh-ud-Din—Heir Mian̉ Muhammad Sultan	Lahore	Rs. 2	〃
37	Ahmad-ud-Din—Yarn Weaver	〃	Rs. 1	〃

№	NAME	RESIDENCE	DONATED	COMMENTS
38	Jamal-ud-Din—Calligrapher	〃	Rs. 1	〃
39	Muhammad Ā'ẓam—Calligrapher	〃	8 annas	〃
40	Saiful Mulook	〃	Rs. 1	〃
41	Miań Sultan Muhammad—Tailor Master	〃	Rs. 3	〃
42	Miań Ghulam Muhammad—Clerk, Press	〃	Rs. 1	〃
43	Muzaffar-ud-Din	〃	Rs. 2	〃
44	Khawaja Mohy-ud-Din—Trader Prime Woollen Cloth	〃	Rs. 1	〃
45	Muhammad Sharif—Student Islamiyyah College	〃	8 annas	〃
46	Abdul Haque—Islamiyyah College	Lahore	Rs. 1	could not be present due to constraints
47	Abdul Majeed—〃	〃	8 annas	〃
48	Ghulam Mohy-ud-Din—Binder, Civil Military Gazette	〃	Rs. 4	〃
49	Taj-ud-Din	〃	Rs. 1	〃
50	Bashir Ahmad	〃	4 annas	〃
51	Nazeer Ahmad	〃	4 annas	〃
52	Karm Ilahi—Doctor	〃	Rs. 5	
53	Sher Muhammad Khan—BA-student	〃	Rs. 1	
54	Ghulam Mohy-ud-Din—BA-student	〃	Rs. 5	

№	NAME	RESIDENCE	DONATED	COMMENTS
55	Sher Ali—BA-student	〃	Rs. 1	
56	Sahibzadah Sirajul-Haque Jamali Nu'mani—Son of the Late Shah Habeebur-Rahman, Sajjaadah Nasheen Chahar Qutb Hansawi, presently visiting Qadian	Sarsawa	½ anna	
57	Qazi Muhammad Yusuf Ali Nu'mani, with family—Sergeant Police, Junaid State, progeny of Ḥaḍrat Imām Ā'ẓam	Tosam, Distt. Hisar	Rs. 10	
58	Sheikh Faizullah Khalidi al-Qureshi—Assistant Inspector	Nabah State	Rs. 1	could not attend
59	Sayyed Nāsir Nawab Delhawi—Pensioner	Qadian	Rs. 2	
60	Mir Muhammad Ismail—Student Islamiyyah College, Lahore	〃	Rs. 2	
61	Muhammad Ismail Sarsawi—Student	〃	½ anna	
62	Sheikh Abdur-Raheem—new Muslim 〃	〃	½ anna	
63	Sheikh Abdur-Rahman—new Muslim 〃	〃	½ anna	
64	Sheikh Abdul Aziz—new Muslim 〃	〃	½ anna	
65	Khuda Yar—new Muslim 〃	〃	½ anna	
66	Gulab-ud-Din—Shawl Weaver	〃	½ anna	
67	Ismail Beig—Pressman	〃	½ anna	
68	Imam-ud-Din	〃	½ anna	

№	NAME	RESIDENCE	DONATED	COMMENTS
69	Sahibzadah Iftikhar Ahmad Ludhianwi	Qadian	½ anna	
70	Sahibzadah Manzoor Muhammad—〃	〃	½ anna	
71	Sahibzadah Mazhar Qayyum—〃	〃	½ anna	
72	Maulavī Abdur Rahman	Khewal Distt. Jhelum	½ anna	
73	Sayyed Khaseelat Ali Shah—Deputy Inspector	Dinga, Distt. Gujrat	Rs. 9	
74	Sayyed Ameer Ali Shah—Sergeant I	Sialkot	Rs. 4	
75	Hakeem Muhammad-ud-Din—Head Copyist	〃	Rs. 1	
76	Munshi Abdul Aziz—Tailor Master	〃	Rs. 1	
77	Sheikh Fazl Kareem—Perfumer	〃	12 annas	
78	Ghulam Mohy-ud-Din—Timber Trader	〃	½ anna	
79	Sheikh Husain Bakhsh—Tailor	Qadian	½ anna	
80	Abdullah—〃	〃	½ anna	
81	Abdur Rahman—〃	〃	½ anna	
82	Ḥāfiẓ Ahmadullah Khan	〃	½ anna	
83	Karam Dād	〃	½ anna	
84	Sayyed Irshād Ali—Student	Sialkot	½ anna	
85	Maulavī Muhammad Abdullah Khan Wazirabadi—College Instructor	Patiala State	Rs. 1 & 8 annas	

№	NAME	RESIDENCE	DONATED	COMMENTS
86	Ḥāfiẓ Nur Muhammad—Sergeant Platoon No. 4	〃	Rs. 1	
87	Muhammad Yusuf—Wood Carver	〃	Rs. 1	
88	Ḥāfiẓ Malik Muhammad—〃	〃	½ anna	
89	Abdul Hameed—Student	〃	4 annas	
90	Muhammad Akbar Khan Sanauri	〃	½ anna	
91	Khalifah Nur-ud-Din—Books Trader	Jammu State	Rs. 3	
92	Allah Ditta—〃	〃	Rs. 2	
93	Maulavī Muhammad Ṣādiq—Teacher	〃	Rs. 2	
94	Miań Nabi Bakhsh—Darner	Amritsar	Rs. 5	
95	Muhammad Ismail—Trader Woolen Cloth, Katrhah Ahluwalia	Amritsar	Rs. 3	
96	Miań Muhammad-ud-Din—Appeal Writer	Sialkot	Rs. 1	
97	Miań Ilahi Bakhsh—Muhalla Māshkiāń	Gujrat	Rs. 1	
98	Miań Charagh-ud-Din—Katrhah Ahluwalia	Amritsar	Rs. 2	
99	Munshi Rurhah—Court Draftsman	Kapurthalah State	Rs. 2	
100	Munshi Zafar Ahmad—Appeal Writer	〃	Rs. 2	
101	Munshi Rustam Ali—Court Inspector	Gurdaspur	Rs. 4	
102	Nawab Khan	Jammu	Rs. 1	

№	NAME	RESIDENCE	DONATED	COMMENTS
103	Miań Abdul Khaliq—Darner	Amritsar	8 annas	
104	Sheikh Abdul Haque—Contractor	Ludhiana	Rs. 1	
105	Muhammad Hasan—Perfumer	"	Rs. 1	
106	Munshi Muhammad Ibrahim—Coarse Cloth Trader	"	Rs. 1	
107	Mistrī Ḥajī 'Iṣmatullāh	"	Rs. 1	
108	Qazi Khawaja Ali—Horse Carriage Contractor	"	Rs. 5	
109	Maulavī Abu Yusuf Mubarak Ali—Imam Masjid Ṣadr	Sialkot	Rs. 1	
110	Abdul Aziz Khan—Student, son of Abdur Rahman Khan, teacher of Sardar Ayub Khan	Rawalpindi	½ anna	
111	Sheikh Nur Ahmad—Owner Riaz-e-Hind Press	Amritsar	½ anna	
112	Sheikh Zahoor Ahmad—Litho Plate Maker	"	½ anna	
113	Mirza Rasool Beig	Kalanaur Distt. Gurdaspur	½ anna	
114	Ḥāfiẓ Abdur Raheem	Batala	Rs. 1	
115	Dr. Faiz Qadir	"	Rs. 2	
116	Sheikh Muhammad Jān—Trader	Wazirabad	Rs. 5	
117	Munshi Nawab-ud-Din—Teacher	Deena Nagar	½ anna	
118	Khalifah Allah Ditta	"	½ anna	

№	NAME	RESIDENCE	DONATED	COMMENTS
119	Miań Khuda Bakhsh—Tailor	Chhokar, Distt. Gujrat	½ anna	
120	Maulavī Ḥāfiẓ Ahmad-ud-Din—Chak Sikandar	Distt. Gujrat	½ anna	
121	Miań Ahmad-ud-Din—Imam Masjid, Qila Didar Singh	Gujranwala	½ anna	
122	Miań Jamal-ud-Din—Fine Wool Weaver	Sekhwan, Distt. Gurdaspur	Rs. 1	
123	Muhammad Akbar—Contractor	Batala	Rs. 4	
124	Master Ghulam Muhammad—B.A., Teacher	Silakot	Rs. 1 & 8 annas	
125	Miań Bagh Husain	Batala	½ anna	
126	Miań Nabi Bakhsh Panda	〃	Rs. 1	
127	Chaudhry Munshi Nabi Bakhsh—Lambardar	〃	Rs. 5	
128	Maulavī Khan Malik Khewal	Distt. Jhelum	½ anna	
129	Miań Khair-ud-Din—Fine Wool Weaver, Sekhwan	Distt. Gurdaspur	Rs. 1	
130	Hakeem Muhammad Ashraf	Batala 〃	Rs. 1	
131	Sheikh Ghulam Muhammad—Student	Distt. Jalandhar	½ anna	
132	Ḥāfiẓ Ghulam Mohy-ud-Din—Book Binder	Qadian	½ anna	
133	Miań Imam-ud-Din—Fine Wool Weaver	Sekhwan	Rs. 1	

№	NAME	RESIDENCE	DONATED	COMMENTS
134	Allah Din—Bathian	Distt. Gurdaspur	½ anna	
135	Sheikh Abdur Raheem—State Employee	Kapurthalah	Rs. 2	
136	Sheikh Muhammad-ud-Din—Shoe Seller	Jammu	Rs. 2	
137	Muhammad Shah—Contractor	〃	8 annas	
138	Nizam-ud-Din—Storekeeper, Theh Ghulam Nabi	Distt. Gurdaspur	½ anna	
139	Imam-ud-Din—〃	〃	½ anna	
140	Sheikh Faqeer Ali—Landlord 〃	〃	½ anna	
141	Sheikh Sher Ali—〃	〃	½ anna	
142	Sheikh Chiragh Ali—〃	〃	½ anna	
143	Shahab-ud-Din—Storekeeper 〃	〃	½ anna	
144	Munshi Abdul Aziz—Patwari, Sekhwan	〃	½ anna	
145	Miań Qutb-ud-Din—Tailor, Badehcha	〃	½ anna	
146	Miań Sultan Ahmad—Student	Gujrat	½ anna	
147	Sheikh Ameer Bakhsh—Theh Ghulam Nabi	Distt. Gurdaspur	½ anna	
148	Sayyed Nizam Shah—Bazed Chak	〃	½ anna	
149	Ḥāfiẓ Muhammad Husain—Dinga	Distt. Gujrat	½ anna	
150	Bābū Gul Hasan—Clerk Railways Office	Lahore	Rs. 1	

№	NAME	RESIDENCE	DONATED	COMMENTS
151	Ḥāfiẓ Nur Muhammad—Faizullah Chak	Distt. Gurdaspur	½ anna	
152	Hasan Khan—Employee State Artillery	Kapurthalah	½ anna	
153	Mirza Jhanda Beig—Pirowal	Distt. Gurdaspur	½ anna	
154	Muhammad Husain—Student, Madeh	Distt. Amritsar	½ anna	
155	Miań Muhammad Ameer—Kund	Sub-disctrict Khushab	½ anna	
156	Ghulam Muhammad—Student	Amritsar	½ anna	
157	Muhammad Ismail—Theh Ghulam Nabi	Distt. Gurdaspur	½ anna	
158	Sheikh Qutb-ud-Din—Kotla Faqeer	Distt. Jhelum	Rs. 1	
159	Miań Ghulam Husain—Baker in the House of the Promised Messiah	Qadian	8 annas	
160	Miań Maula Bakhsh—Leather Trader, Dinga	Distt. Gujrat	Rs. 3	
161	Qazi Muhammad Yusuf—Qazi Kot	Distt. Gujranwala	Rs. 1	
162	Abdullah—Rice Trader	Lahore	½ anna	
163	Maulavī Ḥāfiẓ Karm-ud-Din—Porhanwala	Distt. Gujrat	Rs. 1	
164	Ḥāfiẓ Ahmad-ud-Din—Tailor, Dinga	"	8 annas	
165	Ibadat Ali Shah—Trader Cotton Pod	Distt. Gurdaspur	½ anna	

№	NAME	RESIDENCE	DONATED	COMMENTS
166	Muhammad Khan—Lambardar, Jassarwal	Distt. Amritsar	Rs. 3	
167	Miań Ilm-ud-Din—Kalosaee	Distt. Gujrat	½ anna	
168	Miań Karam-ud-Din—Dinga	〃	Rs. 1	
169	Sheikh Ahmad-ud-Din—〃	〃	½ anna	
170	Miań Ahmad-ud-Din—〃	〃	½ anna	
171	Miań Muhammad Ṣiddīq—Fine Wool Weaver	Sekhwan	8 annas	
172	Miań Ṣādiq Husain	Patiala State	Rs. 1	
173	Maulavī Faqeer Jamal-ud-Din—Syedwala	Distt. Montgomery	½ anna	
174	Maulavī Abdullah—Thattha Sher Ka	〃	½ anna	
175	Miań Abdul Aziz—Student	Qadian	½ anna	
176	Miań Abdullah—Theh Ghulam Nabi	Distt. Gurdaspur	½ anna	
177	Mehr-ud-Din—Caterer, Lalamusa	Distt. Gujrat	Rs. 2	
178	Karam Din—Caterer 〃	〃	Rs. 2	could not attend
179	Imam-ud-Din—Patwari, Lochib	Distt. Gurdaspur	Rs. 1	
180	Fazl Ilahi—Lambardar, Chak Faizullah	〃	Rs. 1	
181	Ghulam Nabi—〃	〃	Rs. 1	
182	Charagh-ud-Din—Builder, Mandī Karan Village	〃	½ anna	

№	NAME	RESIDENCE	DONATED	COMMENTS
183	Qazi Nemat Ali—Khaṭīb [Imam of the Jami Mosque], Batala	〃	Rs. 1	
184	Ahmad Ali—Lambardar, Chak Wazeer	〃	Rs. 1	
185	Imam-ud-Din—Theh Ghulam Nabi	〃	½ anna	
186	Miań Faqeer—Carpet Weaver, Chak Faizullah	〃	½ anna	
187	Miań Ameer—Carpet Weaver 〃	〃	½ anna	
188	Sheikh Barkat Ali—Storekeeper 〃	〃	½ anna	
189	Barkat Ali—Patwari 〃	〃	½ anna	
190	Miań Imam-ud-Din— 〃	〃	½ anna	
191	Sayyed Ameer Husain—Chak Bazed	Distt. Gurdaspur	½ anna	
192	Sheikh Feroz-ud-Din— 〃	〃	½ anna	
193	Sheikh Sher Ali— 〃	〃	½ anna	
194	Sheikh Ata Muhammad— 〃	〃	½ anna	
195	Sayyed Muhammad Shafi— 〃	〃	½ anna	
196	Umar—Watchman 〃	〃	½ anna	
197	Maulavī Ameer-ud-Din—Muhalla Khojawala	Gujrat	½ anna	
198	Mistrī Muhammad Umar	Jammu	½ anna	
199	Sayyed Wazeer Husain—Bazed Chak	Distt. Gurdaspur	½ anna	
200	Mehrullah Shah—Dodan	〃	½ anna	
201	Sultan Bakhsh—Badecha	〃	½ anna	

№	NAME	RESIDENCE	DONATED	COMMENTS
202	Munshi Abdul Aziz a.k.a. Wazeer Khan—Sub-Overseer	Ballabgarh	Rs. 1	
203	Nur Muhammad—Dhoni	Distt. Montgomery	½ anna	
204	Abdur Rasheed—Syedwala	〃	½ anna	
205	Maulavī Ahmad-ud-Din—Imam Masjid, Nāmdār	Distt. Lahore	½ anna	
206	Ḥāfiẓ Moeen-ud-Din	Qadian	½ anna	
207	Abdul Majeed	Kapurthalah	½ anna	
208	Muhammad Khan	〃	Rs. 2	could not be present due to constraints
209	Maulavī Muhammad Husain—Bhagoraeen	〃	Rs. 2	
210	Nizam-ud-Din—〃	〃	½ anna	
211	Faiz Muhammad—Carpenter	Sialkot	½ anna	
212	Sayyed Gohar Shah—Phero Chichi	Distt. Gurdaspur	½ anna	
213	Hakeem Din Muhammad—Student	Qadian	½ anna	
214	Sheikh Fazl Ilahi—Postman	〃	2 annas	
215	Sultan Muhammad—Bukrala	Distt. Jhelum	½ anna	
216	Allah Dia—Kambo	Distt. Amritsar	½ anna	
217	Sayyed Aalim Shah—Said Mallu Village	Distt. Jhelum	½ anna	

№	NAME	RESIDENCE	DONATED	COMMENTS
218	Mistrī Hasan-ud-Din	Sialkot	½ anna	
219	Miran Bakhsh—Bangle Maker	Batala	½ anna	
220	Mehr Sāńwān—Sekhwan	Distt. Gurdaspur	Rs. 1	
221	Hakeem Jamal-ud-Din—Trader	Qadian	Rs. 1	
222	Muhammad Ismail—Student	〃	½ anna	
223	Muhammad Isḥāq—〃	〃	½ anna	
224	Abdullah Khan—Haryana	Distt. Hoshiarpur	R. 2	
225	Karim Bakhsh Mistrī—Bel Chak	Distt. Gurdaspur	½ anna	
226	Mirza Boota Beig	Qadian	½ anna	
227	Mirza Ahmad Beig	〃	½ anna	
228	Muhammad Hayat	Batala	½ anna	
229	Nur Muhammad—Employee Dr. Faiz Qadir	〃	½ anna	
230	Sheikh Ghulam Muhammad—Trader	Amritsar	½ anna	
231	Barkat Ali—Necha Band	Batala	½ anna	
232	Ghulam Husain—Kakka Zaee	〃	½ anna	
233	Raheem Bakhsh—Shanagar	Jhelum	½ anna	
234	Sheikh Ghulam Ahmad—Imam Masjid, Bharhial	Distt. Sialkot	½ anna	
235	Sheikh Ismail—Imam Masjid Bharhial	〃	½ anna	
236	Sheikh Karim Bakhsh—Kahne Chak	Jammu State	½ anna	

№	NAME	RESIDENCE	DONATED	COMMENTS
237	Sheikh Charagh-ud-Din	"	½ anna	
238	Miań Kannu Teli—Tatla	Distt. Gurdaspur	½ anna	
239	Sheikh Maula Bakhsh—Shoe Trader	Sialkot	Rs. 1	
240	Mirza Nizam-ud-Din	Qadian	½ anna	
241	Sayyed Abdul Aziz	Anbala	½ anna	
242	Maulavī Fazl-ud-Din—Kharian	Distt. Gujrat	Rs. 5	could not be present due to constraints
243	Maulavī Fazl-ud-Din—Khushab	Distt. Shahpur	Rs. 10	"
244	Ḥāfiẓ Rahmatullah—Kiranpur	Distt. Dera Doon	Rs. 2	"
245	Nur-ud-Din—Draftsman Barg Mastri	Jhelum	Rs. 2	"
246	Miań Abdullah—Patwari, Sanori	Patiala State	Rs. 1	"
247	Miań Abdul Aziz—Clerk, Water Office, Juman West	Delhi	Rs. 3	"
248	Dr. Boorhe Khan—Assistant Surgeon	Qasoor	Rs. 20	"
249	Maulavī Muhammad Husain—Madrasah Islamiyyah	Rawalpindi	Rs. 1	"
250	Maulavī Khadim Husain—Islamiyyah School	Rawalpindi	Rs. 1	could not attend
251	Bābū Allah Din—Firus, Lighting Department	"	Rs. 1	"
252	Sayyed Inayat Ali Shah	Ludhiana	Rs. 2 & 5 annas	"

№	NAME	RESIDENCE	DONATED	COMMENTS
253	Munshi Ghulam Haider—Deputy Inspector Police	Narowal	Rs. 10	"
254	Maulavī Ilm-ud-Din	"	Rs. 2	"
255	Munshi Mehram Ali—Clerk Sergeant Police	"	Rs. 2	"
256	Bābū Shah Din—Station Master Deena	Distt. Jhelum	Rs. 4	"
257	Munshi Allah Ditta	Sialkot	Rs 21	could not attend
258	Munshi Fateh Muhammad Buzdar—Postmaster, Layyah	Distt. Dera Ismail Khan	Rs. 1	"
259	Sheikh Ghulam Nabi—Storekeeper	Rawalpindi	Rs. 10	"
260	Munshi Muzaffar Ali—Brother of Maulavī Muhammad Ahsan Amrohi	Dera Doon	Rs. 1	"
261	Mian̉ Ahmad Husain—Employee Mian̉ Muhammad Hanif Trader	"	Rs. 1	"
262	Maulavī Muhammad Yaqub	"	Rs. 1	"
263	Munshi Ali Gohar Khan—Branch Postmaster	Jalandhar	Rs. 1	"
264	Munshi Muhammad Ismail—Draftsman, Kalka Railway	Anbala Cantonment	Rs. 5	"
265	Maulavī Ghulam Mustafa—Owner of Shu'la-e-Toor Press	Batala	Rs. 1	"
266	Bābū Muhammad Afzal—Employee Railways, Mombasa	Africa	Rs. 1	"

№	NAME	RESIDENCE	DONATED	COMMENTS
267	Chaudhry Muhammad Sultan—Son of Maulavī Abdul Karim	Sialkot	Rs. 2	"
268	Sayyed Ḥāmid Shah—Acting Superintendent Deputy Commissioner	"	Rs. 2	"
269	Sayyed Hakeem Husam-ud-Din—Chief	"	Rs. 1	"
270	Fazl-ud-Din—Jeweler	"	Rs. 1	"
271	Hakeem Ahmad-ud-Din	"	Rs. 5	"
272	Sheikh Nur Muhammad—Cap Maker	"	Rs. 1	"
273	Muhammad-ud-Din—Patwari, Tarigrhi	Distt. Gujranwala	Rs. 1	"
274	Sayyed Nawab Shah—Instructor	Sialkot	Rs. 1	"
275	Sayyed Charagh Shah	"	Rs. 1	"
276	Chaudhry Nabi Bakhsh—Sergeant Police	Sialkot	Rs. 1	could not attend
277	Muhammad-ud-Din	"	4 annas	"
278	Muhammad-ud-Din—Book Binder	"	8 annas	"
279	Allah Bakhsh	"	4 annas	"
280	Shadi Khan—Trader	Sialkot	Rs. 1	could not attend
281	Chaudhry Allah Bakhsh	"	Rs. 1	"
282	Chaudhry Fateh Din	"	Rs. 1	"
283	Allah Rakha—Shawl Weaver	Batala	Rs. 1	
284	Karam Ilahi—Constable	Ludhiana	Rs. 1	"
285	Peer Bakhsh	"	Rs. 2	"

№	NAME	RESIDENCE	DONATED	COMMENTS
286	Munshi Ilah Bakhsh	Sialkot	Rs. 1	"
287	Karam-ud-Din—Bhupal-wala	"	Rs. 4	"
288	Munshi Karam Ali—Records Clerk	Patiala	Rs. 5	"
289	Mirza Niaz Beig—Officer Canal Department, Rasheedah	Distt. Multan	Rs. 5	"
290	Allah Ditta—Shawl Weaver	Batala	Rs. 1	"
291	Abdul Hakeem Khan—Doctor	Patiala State	Rs. 2	"
292	Azizullah—Sirhindi, Branch Postmaster	Nadoon	Rs. 1	"
293	Nawab Khan—Sub-District Administrator	Jhelum	Rs. 10	"
294	Abdus-Samad—Employee of Nawab Khan listed above	Jhelum	Rs. 1	"
295	Maulavī Nur Muhammad—Trustee [of Nawab Khan listed above]	Distt. Lahore	Rs. 1	"
296	Sayyed Mahdi Hasan—Water Flow Recorder, Lohla Post	"	3 annas	"
297	Maulavī Sher Muhammad—Hijan	Distt. Shahpur	8 annas	"
298	Bābū Nawab-ud-Din—Headmaster, Deenanagar	Distt. Gurdaspur	Rs. 2	
299	Mother of Khair-ud-Din—Sekhwan	"	4 annas	
300	Raheem Bakhsh—Clerk Stable	Sangroor	Rs. 5	could not attend

№	NAME	RESIDENCE	DONATED	COMMENTS
301	Qari Muhammad—Imam Masjid	Jhelum	Rs. 2	〃
302	Sharf-ud-Din—Kotla Faqeer	Distt. Jhe-lum	Rs. 1	Absent
303	Ilm-ud-Din—〃	〃	Rs. 1	〃
304	Maulavī Muhammad Yu-suf—Sanaur	Patiala	Rs. 1 & 13 annas & 1 paisa	〃
305	Ahmad Bakhsh—〃	〃	Rs. 1 & 13 annas & 1 paisa	〃
306	Muhammad Ibraheem—〃	〃	Rs. 1 & 13 annas & 1 paisa	〃
307	Imam-ud-Din—Patwari〃	Lochip Area	Rs. 1	〃
308	Ghulam Nabi a.k.a. Nabi Bakhsh—Faizullah Chak	Distt. Gur-daspur	Rs. 1	〃
309	Munshi Ahmad—Clerk, Government Pen	Patiala	Rs. 1	〃
310	Maulavī Mahmood Hasan Khan—Instructor	〃	4 annas	〃
311	Sheikh Muhammad Hu-sain—Moradabadi	〃	Rs. 1	〃
312	Mistrī Ahmad-ud-Din	Bhera	Rs. 4	〃
313	Mistrī Islam Ahmad	〃	Rs 2	〃
314	Miań Fayyaz Ali	Kapurthal-ah	Rs. 2	〃
315	Miań Sahib Din—Kharian	Distt. Gujrat	Rs. 2	〃
316	Miań Aalam Din—Barber	Bhera	4 annas	〃

№	NAME	RESIDENCE	DONATED	COMMENTS
317	Bābū Karam Ilahi—Deputy Superintendent Mental Hospital, through Sheikh Rahmatullah	Lahore	Rs. 5	//
318	Bābū Ghulam Muhammad	Ludhiana	Rs. 4	//

REMAINDER OF THE NAMES OF THE ATTENDEES OF THE JUBILEE GATHERING

1. Abdur Rahman—new Muslim, Jalandhari. 2. Sayyed Irshad Ali—son of Sayyed Khaseelat Ali Shah, Dinga. 3. Allah Ditta—son of Nur Muhammad, Kamboh. 4. Abdullah—son of Khlaifa Rajab Din, Lahore. 5. Ghulam Muhammad—Student, Dera Bābā Nānak. 6. Roshan Din—Bhera. 7. Allah Widhaya—Pindi Bhattian. 8. Sheikh Ahmad Ali—Chak Bazed. 9. Nur Muhammad—Dhoni. 10. Abdur-Rasheed—Syedwala. 11. Ghulam Qadir—Qadian. 12. Sheikh Ameer—Theh Ghulam Nabi. 13. Ghulam Ghaus—Qadian. 14. Gulab—son of Muhkam, Ahmadabad, District Gurdaspur. 15. Shah Nawaz—Dinga. 16. Eeda—son of Shadi, Qadian. 17. Din Muhammad—Qadian. 18. Sadr-ud-Din—Qadian. 19. Buddha—Qadian. 20. Husaina—Qadian. 21. Imam-ud-Din—Qadian. 22. Khawaja Nur Muhammad—Qadian. 23. Hamid Ali Arāīń—Qadian. 24. Mīrāń Bakhsh—Qadian. 25. Lussoo—Qadian. 26. Faqeer Muhammad—Faizullah Chak. 27. Sheikh Muhammad—Qadian. 28. Khawaja Khewan—Qadian.

29. Sharf Din—Qadian. 30. Fateh Din—Kahaar Dala. 31. Abdullah—Qadian. 32. Labbhoo—Qadian. 32. Lubbha Dogar—Khārā. 33. Nathoo—Qadian. 34. Boota—Qadian.

Translation of the Letter of
Nawab Muhammad Ali Khan, Chief of Maler Kotla
[to Ḥaḍrat Mirza Ghulam Ahmad[as] of Qadian]

بسم الله الرحمٰن الرحيم
نحمده ونصلى علىٰ رسوله الكريم[8]

Respected and Honoured Spiritual Physician, Messiah for the World,

May Allah the Almighty be your Protector. May peace be on you. In compliance with your directive, I submit complete description of the Jubilee celebrations.

Two days, June 21st and 22nd, had been designated for the Jubilee celebrations. We scheduled all activities for the 22nd as the government directive required all activities to be concluded by that date.

The public of Maler Kotla has shown loyalty and fidelity to the government just as its great chiefs have shown loyalty and have provided its proof many times. At times they have supported the government by personally joining a battle. Now that the time of war has passed, we offer any service to the government as circumstances may require and why should we not do this, as this government has bestowed special favours upon us. The Sikhs, during the period of their rule, harassed this state greatly. If General Akhtar Loni had not come in time like a much needed cloud of mercy, this State would have gone from the hands of this family to the

8. In the name of Allah, the Gracious, the Merciful. We praise Him and send blessings on His exalted Prophet[sa]. [Publisher]

hands of the Sikhs. Our family is indebted to the government in every way. This relation has been strengthened because of Your Holiness. The favours of the government on our Community provided the additional incentive for us to do more than our contemporaries.

First: The nearby mosque and our residence were illuminated greatly. A house in my possession outside the town in the village of Sarwani Kote was also illuminated. All the houses were first painted white, lights were fixed in a variety of ways and the following inscription was made on one of the walls:

'God save our Empress.'

There was more lighting at our home compared to most of the remaining city. Due to wind, the illumination could not take place on the 22nd. The whole city was illuminated on the 23rd except for elevated places due to wind.

Second: Three arches. One at the head of the street and two were erected in front of our home. The following inscriptions were written on them in gold. First, at the head of the street, 'Congratulations on the Diamond Jubilee Celebrations.' Second, 'Welcome' was written in English on the door of our house. Finally, on the third arch in front of the house was written, 'Long Live the Empress of India.' A trifle arch was also erected in Sarwani Kot.

Third: At six o'clock in the evening on June 22nd, the members of our Community gathered and prayers were offered in the court of God Almighty for Her Majesty, the Queen and Empress of India, her empire and her long life. We prayed that may God Almighty favour her as she has favoured us and may He include her among the believers, that is, may she benefit from the sun of Islam.

Fourth: I had notified the members of our Community that even those with the least means should illuminate not less than one hundred lights. They can get the funds from me if they cannot afford to do so themselves. I provided funds to five members and the remaining arranged illuminations themselves.

Fifth: I ordered my grantees in Sarwani Kot to arrange illuminations, to which they complied. It is such an exceptional occurrence that it probably did not happen in any other village of the state.

Sixth: On June 23rd, fireworks were launched in celebrations.

Seventh: A feast was arranged for respected friends on the evening of June 22nd.

Eighth: Grain and cash was distributed among the less affluent on the 23rd.

Ninth: There is a suggestion to establish a memorial. I will relate further after a decision has been taken in this respect.

Writer,

Muhammad Ali Khan
Maler Kotla
June 25, 1897

Note: We have made an effort to list the names of everyone. If one or two are left out, it is due to human error.

Printed at the Ḍiyāul-Islam Press Qadian under the supervision of Hakeem Fazl-ud-Din, Press Owner. June 28,1897

GLOSSARY

Aḥmadiyya Muslim Jamā'at—The Community of Muslims who have accepted the claims of Ḥaḍrat Mirza Ghulam Ahmad[as] of Qadian as the Promised Messiah and Mahdi. The Community was established by Ḥaḍrat Mirza Ghulam Ahmad[as] in 1889, and is now under the leadership of his fifth *khalīfah*—Ḥaḍrat Mirza Masroor Ahmad (may Allah be his help). The Community is also known as **Jamā'at-e-Aḥmadiyya**. A member of the Community is called an **Aḥmadī Muslim** or simply an **Aḥmadī**.

Alḥamdolillāh—A phrase from the Holy Quran meaning, all praise belongs to Allah alone.

Allah—Allah is the personal name of God in Islam. To show proper reverence to Him, Muslims often add *Ta'ālā*, translated here as 'the Exalted', when saying His Holy name.

Al-Imam al-Mahdi—The title given to the Promised Reformer by the Holy Prophet Muhammad[sa]; it means the guided leader.

Āmīn—May Allah make it so.

Currency values—The booklet uses rupees, anna and paisa. Rupee was the main unit of currency in India, anna is 1/16 of a rupee and paisa is 1/4 of an anna.

Ḥaḍrat—A term of respect used for a person of established righteousness and piety.

Holy Prophet[sa]—A term used exclusively for the Founder of Islam, Ḥaḍrat Muhammad, may peace and blessings of Allah be upon him.

Holy Quran—The Book sent by Allah for the guidance of mankind. It was revealed word by word to the Holy Prophet Muhammad[sa] over a period of twenty-three years.

Ḥuḍūr—Your Holiness; His Holiness.

Jihad—The literal meaning of this word is 'striving'. The term is used to mean self-purification as well as religious wars in some instances.

Jizyah— The tax that is taken from the free non-Muslim subjects of a Muslim government whereby they ratify the compact that ensures them protection or because it is a compensation for the protection which is guaranteed to them, the non-Muslim subject being free from military service. (*Dictionary of the Holy Quran*, by Malik Ghulam Farid, p. 136)

Mahdi—The literal translation of this word is 'the guided one'. This is the title given by the Holy Prophet Muhammad[sa] to the awaited Reformer of the Latter Days.

Muhammad—Proper name of the Prophet of Islam.

Maulānā or Maulavī—A Muslim religious cleric.

The Promised Messiah—This term refers to the Founder of the Aḥmadiyya Muslim Jamā'at, Ḥaḍrat Mirza Ghulam Ahmad[as] of Qadian. He claimed that he had been sent by Allah in accordance with the prophecies of the Holy Prophet[sa] about the coming of *al-Imam al-Mahdi* (the Guided Leader) and Messiah.

Ra'īs—A term in Urdu language referring to the Chief, having authority over a certain area.

Sūrah—A term in Arabic referring to a chapter of the Holy Quran.

INDEX

Lightning Source UK Ltd.
Milton Keynes UK
UKHW020638210921
390952UK00013B/808

9 781848 800779